T0311445

Cambridge Elements ≡

Elements in New Religious Movements
Series Editor
Rebecca Moore
San Diego State University
Founding Editor
†James R. Lewis
Wuhan University

THE NEW WITCHES
OF THE WEST

Tradition, Liberation, and Power

Ethan Doyle White
Independent Researcher

CAMBRIDGE
UNIVERSITY PRESS

Shaftesbury Road, Cambridge CB2 8EA, United Kingdom

One Liberty Plaza, 20th Floor, New York, NY 10006, USA

477 Williamstown Road, Port Melbourne, VIC 3207, Australia

314–321, 3rd Floor, Plot 3, Splendor Forum, Jasola District Centre, New Delhi – 110025, India

103 Penang Road, #05–06/07, Visioncrest Commercial, Singapore 238467

Cambridge University Press is part of Cambridge University Press & Assessment, a department of the University of Cambridge.

We share the University's mission to contribute to society through the pursuit of education, learning and research at the highest international levels of excellence.

www.cambridge.org
Information on this title: www.cambridge.org/9781009472838

DOI: 10.1017/9781009472852

When citing this work, please include a reference to the DOI 10.1017/9781009472852

First published 2024

A catalogue record for this publication is available from the British Library.

ISBN 978-1-009-47283-8 Hardback
ISBN 978-1-009-47282-1 Paperback
ISSN 2635-232X (online)
ISSN 2635-2311 (print)

The New Witches of the West

Tradition, Liberation, and Power

Elements in New Religious Movements

DOI: 10.1017/9781009472852
First published online: January 2024

Ethan Doyle White
Independent Researcher

Author for correspondence: Ethan Doyle White, ethan-doyle-white@
hotmail.co.uk

Abstract: The terms "witch" and "witchcraft" have been used to mean many different things over the years. In the twentieth century, some people began referring to themselves as witches and espousing esoteric new religions that they called witchcraft. Some of these new religions – most notably Wicca – were forms of modern Paganism, devoted to the veneration of ancient divinities. Others constituted types of Satanism or Luciferianism, embracing the early modern idea of the witch as a Devil worshipper. Recent years have seen growing numbers of Black Americans who practice African diasporic religions adopt the term "witch" too. This Element explores why the image of the witch is so appealing to numerous people living in modern Western countries, examining how witchcraft offers people a connection to the past, a vehicle for liberation, and a means of empowering themselves in an often-troubling world.

Keywords: Witchcraft, Wicca, Satanism, Paganism, Magic

ISBNs: 9781009472838 (HB), 9781009472821 (PB), 9781009472852 (OC)
ISSNs: 2635-232X (online), 2635-2311 (print)

Contents

Introduction

Living in modern Western societies, we are surrounded by witches. People put on pointy hats and dress up as them at Halloween. They tell their children fairy tales about how witches live in gingerbread houses, or sit them down in front of films about schools of witchcraft and wizardry. Some folk enjoy horror movies in which witches butcher students out in the woods; others prefer to read fantasy novels about witches flying through the air. Historians write books about people who were accused of being witches centuries ago, while activists campaign for memorials and pardons for these long-dead individuals. Allegations of witch-like Satanists continue to enthral conspiracy theorists, and politicians complain that they are the victims of witch hunts. Amidst all this, hundreds of thousands of people openly declare themselves to be witches – that being a witch is their religious identity. How can we make sense of all this? What does it all mean? Which witch is which?

The words 'witch' and 'witchcraft' have a very long history in the English language, one stretching right back to the Early Middle Ages. As is the case with many words, their meanings have changed and broadened over time, with different people using them to mean different things. We now have a situation where, as noted by historian Ronald Hutton (2017: ix–x), there are four broad meanings of the term 'witch' in circulation. Each of these meanings in turn has its own complexities and subtypes, thus resulting in the incredibly varied and quite confusing array of different ideas about what a witch can be in the modern world.

The first (and probably the oldest) of these meanings is that the witch is a malevolent person who harms others through the manipulation of supernatural forces. This is the witch who practises *maleficium*, who curses, hexes, or bewitches people and their property. This is what the term 'witch' would have meant to the vast majority of folk in England from the early medieval period right through to the nineteenth century. Despite having their own word for these individuals, the English were certainly not unique in believing in such evildoers; to the French, they were *sorcières*, to Germans *hexen*, to Spaniards *brujas*, and so forth. More broadly, societies throughout recorded history and across the world have believed in witches of this type, giving them names from their own native languages. Sometimes, as a result of colonialism, they have also embraced English and other European terms; the Mapuche people of Chile and Argentina, for instance, adopted the Spanish *brujería* as a synonym for their indigenous word *kalkutun* (Bacigalupo 2007: 20–1).

As malefactors, witches of this sort have typically been feared and hated, and people accused of witchcraft have often been persecuted or killed, a situation that continues in many countries today. Across Europe and the European colonies in the Americas, witch persecutions reached their height in the sixteenth and seventeenth centuries, the early modern period, at a time when these societies increasingly viewed the witch as a Satanist, a figure who travelled to the witches' sabbath to worship the Devil, desecrate the Christian Eucharist, and engage in incestuous orgies. (For good overviews of early modern witch trials see Scarre and Callow 2001; Levack 2016.) Although these European trials effectively ended by the eighteenth century, fears about malicious witchcraft remained part of folk belief in many regions of the Western world well into the twentieth century (Favret-Saada 1980; Davies 2013; Waters 2019; Black 2020). In more recent decades, Westerners have also become accustomed to the malicious witch as a staple of horror cinema, a figure familiar from the likes of *Suspiria* (1977), *The Blair Witch Project* (1999), and *The Witch* (2015). Moreover, early modern fears about secretive Satanic groups, sometimes referred to as witches, have repeatedly resurfaced as conspiracy theories, most famously in the Satanic Panic of the 1980s and early 1990s (Victor 1993; Introvigne 2016: 372–461) and the QAnon phenomenon of the late 2010s and 2020s.

The second meaning of the word 'witch' is far broader and refers to a person who uses supernatural forces either to harm or to help. In this sense, a witch can be either malevolent or benevolent; it is their possession and use of unusual power, not their code of ethics, that defines them. This was a meaning employed primarily by those writing with an explicitly Christian agenda – whether medieval Catholic clergymen or later Protestant reformers – and largely reflected their desire to condemn people engaged in forms of healing, divination, and fortune-telling outside of an ecclesiastical remit, often because they thought these individuals were indirectly reliant on the powers of demons. Only in the nineteenth century does it appear that this broader meaning of the word 'witch' gained wider use among the English population. Thus, the term 'witch' could be applied to figures more commonly known as cunning folk, individuals who dealt professionally or semi-professionally in healing, in finding lost property, and in helping to lift curses placed by malevolent witches (on the subject of which see Davies 2003). This new meaning came to particular prominence in popular culture. When American writer L. Frank Baum (1856–1919) published his successful children's book *The Wonderful Wizard of Oz* in 1900, he portrayed a fictional universe containing both Good Witches of the North and South, and Wicked Witches of the East and West (Baum 1900). Witches who are benevolent or morally ambiguous have since become a staple of fantasy fiction, promoted through the writings of Terry Pratchett (1948–2015), Philip Pullman (b. 1946), and J. K. Rowling (b. 1965). Once introduced into the cultural lexicon, this use of the term 'witch' would have major repercussions, opening up the possibility for increasing numbers of people to claim the identity for themselves and to reshape it for their own purposes.

Deriving from the typical European portrayal of malevolent witches as female, the third understanding of 'witch' describes a woman who is rebellious, strong-willed, anti-social, or otherwise independent of male domination. Gaining particular traction in the twentieth century, this use of the term has often been thrown at women in a derogatory and sometimes misogynistic fashion. Thus, amid her unsuccessful campaign to win the 2016 US presidential election, Hillary Clinton (b. 1947) was repeatedly cast as 'the Wicked Witch of the Left' by her critics. Three years prior, opponents of former British prime minister Margaret Thatcher (1925–2013) campaigned to get the song 'Ding-Dong! The Witch Is Dead' to the top of the pop charts following the announcement of her death. At the same time, this highly gendered use of 'witch' could also be embraced as an expressly feminist statement. As shall be highlighted later in this Element, various feminist activists have openly declared themselves to be witches and emphasised their sympathy for the victims of the early modern witch trials – even to the extent of campaigning to have these victims memorialised near their places of execution.

The fourth and final definition of the word 'witch' is that which concerns us most here. It encompasses those I call *modern religious witches*, people who adopt the identity of the witch for themselves in reference to their own ritual practices and spiritual beliefs. This term refers not to a single phenomenon but to a cluster of different traditions, most of which can be considered new religious movements as well as forms of esotericism and occultism. These new religions have almost entirely arisen within Western countries, especially those in the Anglosphere, since the early part of the twentieth century. As pointed out by Brian P. Levack, a historian specialising in the early modern witch trials, modern Western witchcrafts are 'qualitatively different from the witchcraft that was actually practised ... in the past' (Levack 2016: 267). Indeed, prior to the twentieth century it seems that very few people would have wanted to consider themselves a witch; the label of 'witch' was almost always an accusation made against other people, one that could have very serious repercussions. That 'witch' has become a term people embrace for themselves illustrates the extent of the sociocultural transformations that Western societies have undergone since the seventeenth century.

By far the largest and best known of these modern witchcraft religions is Wicca, a modern Pagan tradition that came to public attention in England during the 1950s, largely thanks to the efforts of the English 'Father of Wicca' Gerald Gardner (1884–1964). He and other early Wiccans claimed that they were practitioners of a religion that stretched back deep into the pre-Christian past, adding that it was the adherents of this tradition who had been persecuted in the early modern witch trials. Wicca soon spread abroad, forming what Hutton has termed 'the first fully formed religion which England has given the world' (Hutton 2019: vii). However, Wicca was not the only group embracing the identity of the witch in this period. In 1928, a few Oxford University students briefly played at being witches (Wheeler 2018), and it is quite possible that other small witchcraft groups emerged in the first half of the twentieth century but left little or no trace in the historical record. From the 1960s, there were also various British esotericists who insisted that it was they, rather than Gardner's Wiccans, who were the true inheritors of historical witchcraft traditions. The best known of these was Robert Cochrane (1931–1966), who operated a group to the west of London in the early to mid-part of that decade. Cochrane's writings posthumously circulated in a milieu whose practitioners increasingly labelled themselves 'traditional witches', a designation that became particularly popular from the 1990s (Doyle White 2018a). Some of these traditional witches, such as the Essex-based Andrew D. Chumbley (1967–2004), practised Luciferian traditions (on which see Gregorius 2013), while others pursued forms of traditional witchcraft that were effectively types of eclectic Wicca.

Esotericists in the United States also took an interest in witchcraft. Jack Parsons (1914–1952), the California-based rocket scientist committed to the new religion of Thelema, established a group he called The Witchcraft in 1950 (Hedenborg White 2019). The imagery of early modern witchcraft was also absorbed into LaVeyan Satanism, a new religion established by another California occultist, Anton LaVey (1930–1997), through the formation of his Church of Satan in 1966 (Introvigne 2016: 299–328; Laycock 2023). Meanwhile, the 1960s saw Wicca spread rapidly through the United States, where the influence of social movements like second-wave feminism resulted in the formation of a varied range of different Wiccan traditions (Clifton 2006). During the 1990s, growing Wiccan influence on popular depictions of witchcraft, especially television series like *Buffy the Vampire Slayer* and *Charmed*, fuelled the rise of a teenage Wiccan subculture (Berger and Ezzy 2007; Johnston and Aloi 2007), while the 2010s saw interest in witchcraft again spike among young people, this time driven heavily by social media outlets like TikTok and Instagram (Orrell 2019; Miller 2022). The 2010s also saw growing utilisation of the term 'witch', alongside the Spanish synonym *bruja*, among Black Americans practising certain African diasporic religions.

Although a growing body of scholarship on these modern witchcraft religions has appeared, especially since the turn of the twenty-first century, in general there has been little comparative analysis between them. Among the groups discussed here, Wicca and LaVeyan Satanism have attracted the most attention, but rarely, if ever, have scholars considered them in tandem. This may be owing in part to a tendency among modern Pagans (and some of the scholars who research them) to try to distance themselves from Satanism (Doyle White 2018b: 142–3). This, in turn, is often tied in with conflicts over the identity of the witch, as practitioners of different new religions insist that they legitimately use the term, while their rivals are mere pretenders. One prominent American Wiccan writer, for instance, related that 'many Satanists call themselves Witches, even though they are not' (Grimassi 2000: 252). A common claim among Wiccans is that Satanists are merely 'reverse Christians', for they draw the figure of Satan from Christian mythology rather than turning to altogether non-Christian sources of inspiration (for instance Starhawk 1987: 7, 345). Conversely, Satanists have thrown this accusation back at Wiccans. LaVey referred to Wiccans disparagingly as 'pseudo-Christian groups' who 'base seventy-five per cent of their philosophy on the trite and hackneyed tenets of Christianity' (LaVey 2005: 51). Perhaps because they compete for control over the same images, iconography, and identity, there is often little love lost between different forms of modern religious witchcraft.

The New Witches of the West seeks to explore these varied new religions in tandem, emphasising the commonalities that can be seen across them, rather than the differences that they often wish to emphasise. In doing this, it pursues a particular theme: what is it about the idea of witchcraft and the identity of the witch that appeals to people living in modern Western societies? It thus endeavours to offer new perspectives not only on the construction of new religions but also on the cultural history of witchcraft itself.

1 Tradition

Scholars have long recognised that one of the key ways in which new religions seek to legitimate their existence is by appealing to the power of the past. The patina of time lends a sense of authenticity to religion, rendering a particular belief or practice worthy of respect in the eyes of many observers. Scholars of religion can be just as prone to displaying this sort of sentiment as other people; academics attending conferences are not often observed laughing when presented with the teachings of Zoroastrianism and Judaism, and yet have been seen doing so when informed of the beliefs held by Scientologists (Thomas 2022) and Raëlians (Chryssides 2003: 45). Evidently, the perceived age of a religion has an impact on the extent to which many people will take it seriously.

The scholar of new religions James R. Lewis recognised this important point when he described the 'appeal to tradition' as being one of three main legitimation strategies employed by new religious movements (Lewis 2003: 14). While the sources of tradition from which a new religion may draw can certainly vary, from notions of primordial wisdom to historical texts, they nevertheless all illustrate that practitioners of new religions repeatedly feel that a link with the past is what makes their practice relevant in the present. This can operate on a personal, psychological level, but also on a broader sociological one, as a religious minority seeks wider influence, respect, or simply toleration.

Witchcraft is particularly pertinent on this count because it offers the potential for an appeal to the past par excellence. Indeed, there are few concepts in the Western cultural imagination that so readily evoke an association with bygone eras. One can see this attitude, for example, in various British novels from the early to mid-twentieth century. Gerald Gardner introduced his 1949 novel *High Magic's Aid* with the statement 'Witchcraft! Stuff and nonsense. No one believes in such things nowadays' (Gardner 1999: 9). Similarly, in his 1934 novel *The Devil Rides Out*, Dennis Wheatley (1897–1977) had one of his characters declare that they do not believe in witchcraft because 'nobody does in these days' (Wheatley 1970: 29). In the 1930 detective novel *The Secret of High Eldersham* by Miles Burton (a pen name of Cecil Street, 1884–1964), one character announces that 'the witch-cult, in this country at any rate, is supposed to have ceased centuries ago' (Burton 2016: 80), while Agatha Christie's (1890–1976) 1961 novel *The Pale Horse* featured the statement 'there aren't any witches nowadays' (Christie 1990: 43). Witchcraft, and a belief in witchcraft, was repeatedly presented as a thing of the past, at least in those parts of the world where modern religious witches first appeared.

Arguably, this sense of the essential 'pastness' of witchery is not something intrinsic to it as a topic, but instead reflects the way in which discourses about witchcraft have been shaped in modern Western societies. As historian Jan Machielsen (2021: 1–4) has pointed out, the notion that a belief in witchcraft fundamentally belongs to the past was something that scholars writing on the subject deliberately promoted from the eighteenth century onwards, even when that meant overlooking the continued perpetuation of said beliefs. In turn, this view of witchcraft can be seen as just one facet of the broader discourse about the so-called disenchantment of modernity, through which European and European colonial elites sought to consign what they called 'magical' and 'superstitious' beliefs and practices to history by presenting them as fundamentally pre-modern (on which see Josephson-Storm 2017). In this social context, to believe in witchcraft became an increasingly stigmatised position in many European communities. Thus, from at least the nineteenth century onwards it would be common for people to insist that while their forebears had believed in witchcraft, they themselves did not – even if, on further investigation, it sometimes turned out that their professed disbelief was not always sincere (for instance Favret-Saada 1980: 16; Mencej 2017: 40).

For those founders of new religions who, in the twentieth century, declared themselves witches, it was witchcraft's sense of pastness that allowed them to portray themselves as the inheritors of a genuinely historic tradition. Witchcraft also offered the advantage of being a subject about which there was still a considerable aura of mystery, a mystery that would allow for different interpretations as to its historical nature among modern religious witches. The dominant scholarly understanding of European witchcraft throughout the nineteenth century, and up to the middle of the twentieth, had been what later historians have termed the Rationalist school of thought (Monter 1972: 435–6; Fudge 2006: 490). This approach regarded historical European belief in witchcraft as a delusion and often argued that ecclesial authorities had exploited this belief to cement their own power and dominance. Arising in contrast to this interpretation was the Romantic school, the adherents of which believed that a religion of witches had really existed in late medieval and early modern Europe. This school of thought nevertheless broke down into factions, some deeming these historical witches to have been Satanists and others regarding them as representatives of a surviving pre-Christian religion. Unsurprisingly, given their belief in the historical reality of a witchcraft religion, it was the perspectives of these Romantic scholars that would ultimately prepare the ground for the emergence of modern religious witchcraft.

The Emergence of Wicca

Of the various new religions that claim the identity of the witch, none is better known than Wicca. Indeed, the number of Wiccans is now in the hundreds of thousands (Doyle White 2016a: 164–6), meaning that they probably represent the single largest group of self-described witches in the world today. Wicca is unusual among new religions in that, to a significant extent, it represents an outgrowth of an idea originally advanced by historians and other scholars. The idea in question was that the people accused and often executed during the early modern witch trials had been neither committed Devil worshippers nor innocents caught up in the delusions of their persecutors; rather, they had been members of a surviving pre-Christian religious tradition devoted to the worship of a horned god.

As historian Norman Cohn (1975: 103–4) highlighted, the origins of this theory can be traced to Karl Ernst Jarcke (1801–1852), a professor of criminal law at the University of Berlin. In 1828 Jarcke added his own comments to the records of a seventeenth-century German witch trial that he was editing for publication. There, he suggested that the early modern witches had been adherents of a real Devil-worshipping religion, but that it had originated as a pre-Christian Germanic tradition that had morphed into Satanism only after being demonised as such by the Christian clergy. The idea was then adapted by Franz Josef Mone (1796–1871), the director of the Baden archives, who in 1839 argued that the witches' cult had originated as a secretive religion devoted to the god Dionysus, brought into the Germanic world by slaves. As Cohn (1975: 105) observed, both Jarcke and Mone were practising Roman Catholics and were hostile to the witches they described, but there was another historian who took a more sympathetic view, the Frenchman Jules Michelet (1798–1874).

Michelet devoted his 1862 book *La Sorcière* to the topic of European witchcraft. He believed that the witches' sabbaths had originated as pre-Christian ceremonies involving a masked figure representing the god Pan and the lighting of candles for a lunar goddess, but that by the eleventh or twelfth century these rites had transformed into a deliberate mockery of Christian ritual (Michelet 1992: 98–100). Although Michelet's portrayal of the witches' cult was not wholly positive, he nevertheless contrasted it favourably with what he regarded as the abhorrent nature of medieval Europe, casting the Church and the aristocracy as deeply oppressive forces. Michelet's framework was a probable influence on an American writer, Charles Leland (1824–1903), who spent much time in Italy during the closing decades of the nineteenth century. In 1899 Leland published *Aradia or the Gospel of the Witches*, largely an English translation of a text given to him by a Tuscan fortune-teller. Assembling various charms and spells from northern Italian folklore, *Aradia* also contained references to Diana as the goddess of the witches. It was probably this reference to a pre-Christian deity that encouraged Leland's suggestion that the material contained in *Aradia* derived from 'ancient Latin or Etruscan lore' (Leland 1899: 115) and that a witches' cult devoted to Diana had persisted throughout the medieval and early modern periods (Leland 1899: 104).

Despite having circulated for around a century, the theory of a pre-Christian witches' cult would only reach its apogee in the 1920s. The scholar responsible was an Egyptologist, Margaret Murray (1863–1963), who was based at University College London and bore the distinction of having been the first woman in the United Kingdom to be professionally appointed to lecture in archaeology. The start of the First World War had prevented Murray from travelling to Egypt and so she refocussed her attentions on an alternative subject, that of witchcraft in medieval and early modern Europe. She published several articles on the topic before bringing out a book, *The Witch-Cult in Western Europe*, in 1921. Murray embraced the view that the witches perse-cuted in these periods had been members of an ancient pre-Christian religion devoted to a horned god, a figure whom Christians had demonised as the Devil, although she acknowledged that in the distant past this tradition might also have worshipped a 'Mother Goddess' (Murray 1921: 13). She called this religion

'Ritual Witchcraft' and 'the Dianic cult' (Murray 1921: 11–12) and argued that its followers assembled in covens that typically consisted of thirteen members. For Murray, these covens met for specialised ritual meetings termed Esbats as well as for four celebratory assemblies each year, the Sabbaths (Murray 1921: 97). It was in the fifteenth century that persecutions of the witch religion arose, she argued, because it was only then that the Church was sufficiently well established to launch a full assault on its rival (Murray 1952: 22).

Although reviews by other historians highlighted the serious problems underlying Murray's thesis, she was able to popularise her ideas through her entry on witchcraft in the *Encyclopædia Britannica*, which remained in place from 1929 to 1969 (Sheppard 2013: 169). Furthermore, from the 1940s through to the 1970s, a number of other writers promoted and extended her ideas in books aimed at a popular readership, among them Pennethorne Hughes (1952), T. C. Lethbridge (1962), and Michael Harrison (1973). In addition, her ideas were also spread through works of fiction. A good example of this is *The Secret of High Eldersham*, a detective novel from 1930 in which a drug-smuggler helps to cover his criminal activities by forming a witches' coven in an East Anglian village, with one character explicitly referencing Murray's work (discussed in Cowdell 2022).

The Murrayite historical narrative arguably proved the single most important influence on Wicca as it emerged in the middle of the twentieth century. Gerald Gardner, who played a seminal role in organising and promoting the religion from the early 1950s until his death in 1964, claimed to have been initiated into a pre-existing witches' coven operating in the New Forest area of southern England in 1939 (Bracelin 1960: 164–6). There remains a debate among historians as to Gardner's reliability on this count (summarised in Hutton 2019: 213–48), but it is nevertheless significant that his claims to be part of an older tradition were integral to his own presentation of Wicca. Indeed, Gardner built on this claim to present his nascent movement – which he referred to not as 'Wicca' but as 'witchcraft' or the 'Craft of the Wica' (Gardner 1971: 257) – as 'the remnants of a Stone Age religion' (Gardner 1954: 19–20). He nevertheless acknowledged that it was a tradition that had undergone change throughout the millennia, for instance proposing that it had been influenced by the Greco-Roman mystery religions, and thus by the traditions of ancient Egypt (Gardner 1954: 48, 95). The witch trials intensified when they did, he argued, at the instigation of the papacy, which was concerned about the spread of new ideas imported from the east following the culmination of the Crusades (Gardner 1954: 127–8). He referred to this period of persecution as the 'burning time' (Gardner 1971: 35, 257), although he took the view that the witchcraft religion had nevertheless survived, allowing it to resurface in the more tolerant context of the mid-twentieth century.

Gardner's religion, now called Gardnerian Wicca, was organised through small groups termed covens, into which new members would receive initiation. These groups performed rituals to manipulate etheric forces to specific ends, in addition to celebrating seasonal festivals termed Sabbats. Gardnerian theology revolved around an 'Old Horned God' and a 'Moon Goddess' (Gardner 1971: 22), a duotheistic perspective that was a departure from Murray's ideas but that indicated influences from other sources, like Leland's *Aradia*. Gardnerian Wicca provided the template for other groups that emerged from the 1950s onwards, thus facilitating the establishment of Wicca as a broader religious movement composed of multiple variants, typically called traditions. Gardner's general narrative of Wicca as a surviving ancient religion would be repeated in the publications and media outreach of many other prominent Wiccans during the 1960s and 1970s, including Doreen Valiente (1922–1999), Patricia Crowther (b. 1927), and Alex Sanders (1926–1988), the last of whom used the Gardnerian liturgy as the basis for his own Alexandrian Wicca. The narrative became something like an orthodoxy within the Wiccan community, representing what historian James W. Baker called 'the Witch Party Line' (Baker 1996: 171).

Outside observers could (and did) conclude that people like Gardner were consciously making false claims about their links to historic witchcraft traditions, and thus engaging in deliberate deception. This, however, would discount the important role that reincarnation probably played in the worldview of early Wiccans. Gardner was a professed believer in reincarnation (Gardner 1954: 18), according it a prominent role in his first novel, *A Goddess Arrives*; he also suggested that the coven members who initiated him had reported memories of past lives during which they had been witches (Gardner 1971: 11, 14). Moreover, various early Wiccans may have had other experiences that would have served as personal confirmation of the Murrayite theory. Valiente, for example, claimed to have received psychic communications from the spirit of a witch who had been part of a coven active in Surrey during the eighteenth or early nineteenth century (Valiente 1989: 99–116). It seems probable that, for many Wiccans, such experiences played an important role in offering confirmation of the Murrayite interpretation and thus affirming their faith in the genuine antiquity of their religion.

One of the tactics employed by the early Wiccans to emphasise the historical origins of their tradition was the use of mock-archaic and deliberately antiquated terminology. Gardner called one of his earliest ritual texts 'Ye Bok of Ye Art Magical' and presented documents, almost certainly written by himself, that he claimed had been inherited from generations past. One of the core rituals in his liturgy became known as 'drawing down the moon', which was a reference to an alleged rite performed by the witches of ancient Thessaly (Doyle White 2021a). The term 'Wicca', which was increasingly used for the religion as a whole by the 1960s, drew upon the Old English term for witch, *wicca* (Doyle White 2010), while the religion's most common ethical tenet became known as the Wiccan Rede, adopting the latter word as a deliberate archaism (Doyle White 2015). Early Wiccans also adopted prehistoric sites such as the Rollright Stones on the Oxfordshire–Warwickshire border as places to perform certain rituals, further underscoring the connection they perceived between themselves and peoples of the past (Doyle White 2014).

As previously noted, the severe problems with the Murrayite theory had already been highlighted by specialists in the early modern witch trials, and there were certainly works published concomitantly with Murray's that remained committed to the Rationalist interpretation of the subject (for instance Robbins 1959). Nevertheless, Murray's ideas attracted considerable interest and support, especially among non-specialist readers. In 1962, Canadian historian Elliot Rose could complain that those whom he called 'the Murrayites seem to hold, at the time of writing, an almost undisputed sway at the higher intellectual levels' (Rose 1962: 14). Rose set out to highlight the underlying errors permeating Murray's ideas in his book *A Razor for a Goat*, although he still maintained the real existence of early modern witches' covens, thus situating himself within the Romantic school of witchcraft historiography. Putting forward an idea akin to that of Jarcke and Michelet, he suggested that European witch cults had pre-Christian origins but were reformed into a more standardised Satanic movement from the thirteenth century onwards by members of the Goliards, a group of wandering scholars disillusioned with the Church (Rose 1962: 167–8). Rose acknowledged Gardner's assertions, and seemed to accept the possibility that the coven Gardner claimed to have discovered was a descendant of a far older witchcraft, but considered the modern Pagan elements and Goddess worship to have been added no earlier than 1880 and probably after 1930 (Rose 1962: 202–6).

The 1960s has been seen as the start of a revolution in witchcraft historiography (Fudge 2006: 491). Historians publishing on the topic in this decade often saw a clear distinction between their work and what had gone before; in 1964, for instance, Spanish historian Julio Caro Baroja declared that up to three-quarters of earlier writings on witchcraft should just be dismissed (Baroja 2001: 242–3). Unlike both the Rationalists who derided early modern witchcraft beliefs as delusions manipulated by social elites, and the Romantics who believed that witch cults had really existed, the new generation of scholars was informed by approaches from the social sciences. As well as drawing on new perspectives from social psychology, anthropology, and sociology, these scholars were often open to the broader study of the cultural backgrounds from which witchcraft accusations emerged (Fudge 2006: 491). Over the course of the 1960s and 1970s, important monographs were produced by a range of historians, notably Alan Macfarlane (b. 1941), Keith Thomas (b. 1933), H. C. Erik Midelfort (b. 1942), Norman Cohn (1915–2007), Richard Kieckhefer (b. 1946), and Gustav Henningsen (b. 1934). By focussing on different facets of the early modern witch trials in increasing detail, they collectively demonstrated not only that there had been no organised cult of witches to begin with but also that earlier Rationalist interpretations had been overly simplistic regarding why and how the trials took place.

It was thus in the 1960s and 1970s, the period when Wicca was beginning to establish itself as a recognisable alternative religion in Britain and the United States, that scholarly books began to appear that seriously undermined the historical narrative around which it had been constructed. For many Wiccans, the Murrayite origin story was the crux on which the validity of their tradition rested; if Wicca was not the survival of an ancient witches' religion, they reasoned, it was not worth devoting one's life to. Baker was fascinated by Wicca, and met with Sanders, but later reported a 'galling' feeling after realising that he 'had been deceived by its historical claims' (Baker 1996: 172). New Zealand Wiccan Ben Whitmore similarly described 'one rather sad conversation' with a young couple who were abandoning Wicca because their reading on witchcraft history had 'convinced them they were living a lie' (Whitmore 2010: 3).

How widespread this approach was is unclear. Many British Wiccans – especially in more highly educated and middle-class corners of the community – certainly came to terms with the idea that theirs was a new religion during the 1980s, and did not see this as sufficient reason to abandon Wicca altogether. As the anthropologist Tanya Luhrmann noted, based on her research with an English Wiccan coven in this period, some practitioners recognised 'the factual falsehood' of the traditional narrative yet 'embrace[d] the historical claim as a metaphorical truth' (Luhrmann 1989: 242). Similarly, Ronald Hutton recounted attending a seminar at King's College London in 1990 at which senior British Wiccans declared, 'one by one, that [Wicca's] traditional historiography should be regarded as myth and metaphor rather than as literal history' (Hutton 2003: 265). Hutton subsequently wrote his own history of Wicca's emergence, *The Triumph of the Moon* (Hutton 1999; revised Hutton 2019), a work 'written not to demolish a belief system but to fill a vacuum created by the collapse of one' (Hutton 2010: 241).

Hutton's book received a mixed reception. Many in the academic community were clearly unsympathetic to the idea of investigating Wicca to begin with, and

Hutton found that his career progression stalled for around a decade after publication (Doyle White and Feraro 2019: 8). On the other hand, historians and other scholars with an interest in new and alternative religions rallied around *Triumph* as a classic; thus far, both Hutton and his book have been honoured in two edited volumes (Evans and Green 2009; Feraro and Doyle White 2019) and a special issue of the journal *Magic, Ritual, and Witchcraft*. Among Wiccans and other Pagans, the book's impact was 'felt strongly', allowing the anthropologist Helen Cornish to observe a 'Huttonisation' in how practitioners perceived their history (Cornish 2009: 18). While some embraced *Triumph* – and Hutton has become a much-loved figure across substantial portions of the Pagan community – others have reacted quite aggressively against his work. Cornish noted that many Pagans felt that Hutton was promoting 'a sense of absolute rupture and discontinuity' between historical witchcraft and Wicca (Cornish 2009: 19), despite the fact that he has repeatedly highlighted areas of Wiccan continuity with the past, especially through the traditions of ceremonial magic (Hutton 1995: 4; 2003: 87).

Evidently, there are still many Wiccans who continue to believe some version of the Murrayite theory, and who, following Hutton (2011), can perhaps be termed 'counter-revisionists' for their opposition to the revisionist witchcraft historiography of the 1960s onwards. For some of these individuals, this belief is simply a matter of faith, and they take little interest in seeking historical evidence for it or challenging historians. In some cases they have repeated the Murrayite narrative in their writings, occasionally putting their own spin on it. The American Wiccan Raven Grimassi (Gary Erbe, 1951–2019), whose efforts went into promoting an Italian-flavoured variant of the religion that he called Stregheria, for instance claimed that Aradia, the eponymous daughter of Diana in Leland's *Gospel*, was actually a fourteenth-century witch who helped to revive the Murrayite religion (Grimassi 2000). Grimassi was clearly defensive when it came to attacks on his claims to long-term historical continuity, maintaining that his critics were simply those 'so unsure of their own spirituality that they feel the need to dismantle another's' (Grimassi 2000: 260).

Rather than simply ignoring mainstream historical scholarship, a handful of Wiccans have sought to challenge it more directly, typically through Pagan magazines, online blogs, and in one case a self-published book. Most of this has not addressed the broad array of historians who have published on early modern witchcraft beliefs since the 1960s, but instead has targeted Hutton specifically, presumably because he is the only professional historian to have devoted significant attention to Wicca's emergence and thus has become a prominent figure against whom Wiccan counter-revisionists can rally. These criticisms of Hutton often come across as being emotionally charged and sometimes obsessive; the professor has noted that on 'rare occasions' they have amounted to 'outright abuse' (Hutton 2003: 279). The most concerted critique was the aforementioned self-published work, written by Whitmore, an Alexandrian Wiccan high priest, and brought out in 2010 (Whitmore 2010). As Hutton observed, Whitmore's work focussed on attacking *Triumph of the Moon* on issues of 'detail, often trivial', apparently to undermine the historian's authority among Pagan readers (Hutton 2010: 253–4). Even though Whitmore wanted to keep open as many possible connections between pre-Christian religions and Wicca as he could, he still acknowledged that he was 'not proposing an alternative history of my own' (Whitmore 2010: 84) and that 'today's witchcraft [i.e. Wicca] is largely a reinvention' (Whitmore 2010: 1). Evidently, the context of witchcraft historiography was such that it was no longer possible for anyone to seriously argue, with support from the available source material, that Wicca was a surviving pre-Christian religion.

Indeed, even among those who came to accept that Wicca was not the continuation of an ancient witches' cult, there was still a deep desire to evoke strong associations with the past. Thus, for instance, in 2012 the prominent English Wiccans Janet Farrar (b. 1950) and Gavin Bone (b. 1964) would refer to Wicca as 'the reconstructed remnants of Western European Shamanism' (Farrar and Bone 2012: 27). In this sense, Wicca – like other modern Pagan religions – has been presented as a revival or reconstruction, rather than a survival, of ancient religion. The appeal of tradition remains incredibly important for many Wiccans, even if they no longer accept the Murrayite narrative around which the religion was originally built.

A Darker Witchcraft

While the Murrayite narrative formed one current within the Romantic tradition of witchcraft historiography, it was not the only one. An alternative perspective, also emerging largely in 1920s Britain, reaffirmed the early modern belief that witches really were Satanists, although then sought to provide this Satanic religion with some sort of historical grounding, one that ultimately looked to the Middle East. The most prominent figure in this tradition of interpretation was Montague Summers (1880–1948), an English convert to Roman Catholicism who wrote prolifically on various subjects, but who is best known for his writings on witchcraft, vampires, and werewolves (see Doherty 2020). For Summers, the witchcraft of medieval and early modern Europe was devoted to 'the worship of the Evil Principle [*sic*], the Enemy of Mankind, Satan' (Summers 1926: 29). In his view, the witches' religion had emerged in Europe from the eleventh century on, and was 'mainly the spawn of Gnostic heresy' (Summers 1926: 29), thus deriving from ideas that originally arose in the Middle East. At the same time, he also acknowledged that this witchcraft was 'in some sense ... a descendant of the old pre-Christian magic' (Summers 1926: 29). Summers was a committed believer in the literal existence of supernatural evil, taking the view that demons could sometimes really appear at the witches' sabbaths (Summers 1926: 8), and thus he seemed to regard the witch trials as a legitimate response to a severe threat facing Christendom.

Although Summers' ideas never had any 'deep impact' on the mainstream historiography of early modern witchcraft (Fudge 2006: 494), their influence can clearly be seen among various esotericists and writers of popular non-fiction. A prominent example of this is the work of Rollo Ahmed (c. 1898–1958), a Guyanese-born esotericist who cultivated the image of himself as an Egyptian mystic while living in Britain (Josiffe 2014). In his 1936 book *The Black Art*, Ahmed wrote derogatorily about medieval and early modern witches, describing them as 'pitiable and disgusting wrecks, half-demented sadists and workers of evil for the love of it' (Ahmed 1971: 72). Ahmed proceeded to trace this witch cult to a Middle Eastern origin, claiming that the Crusades had resulted in 'prisoners of the Saracens' returning to Europe, bringing with them 'theories and practices of Oriental magic, upon which much of the current witchcraft came to be based' (Ahmed 1971: 71). Similar ideas were later articulated by the Indian-born Sufi writer Idries Shah (1924–1996), who wrote on the topic of witchcraft under the nom de plume Arkon Daraul. In his 1961 book *Secret Societies*, Shah rejected the Murrayite perspective and instead argued that the European witches' religion had been 'a devil-worship cult which practised black magic' (Daraul 1961: 166). He proceeded to suggest that this witchcraft had emerged in the Middle Ages as a syncretic blend between 'remnants of folk-belief from pre-Christian times' coupled with a secretive North African religious tradition known as 'two-hornism' (Daraul 1961: 170).

By the early part of the 1960s, there was thus an established tradition of interpretation, especially aimed at a popular market, which emphasised a diabolical witches' religion as having arisen through influences derived ultimately from the Middle East. Although this was primarily articulated by non-academics, there was one professional historian who embraced it, the aforementioned Elliot Rose. Perhaps unsurprisingly, in *A Razor for a Goat* Rose commented that if a form of 'English witchcraft' that was 'less artificial' than Gardner's had survived from earlier centuries, it would likely have 'nothing self-consciously pagan about it' (Rose 1962: 213). It would not be long before individuals making claims to represent just such a tradition began to appear.

In 1964, the year that Gardner died, the Witchcraft Research Association (WRA) was formed in an attempt to unify Britain's self-described witches. However, in contrast to its founders' ideals, the WRA would be only short-lived, as it was swiftly riven by divisions played out in its newsletter, *Pentagram*. The fiercest critic of the Gardnerians within *Pentagram* was Tony Melachrino, a contributor writing under the pseudonym of Taliesin. He claimed to have spent 'some twenty years' in a hereditary tradition (Taliesin 1965b: 19), something transmitted from his mother and aunt (Taliesin 1965a: 9).[1] Casting some doubt on these claims was Valiente's subsequent researches, which led her to seriously question the veracity of his allegations (Valiente 1989: 131–2). Taliesin juxtaposed his own 'ancient' witchcraft against Gardner's 'modern' tradition (Taliesin 1965a: 9), claiming that Gardner's witchcraft was largely the latter's own creation, cobbled together from the writings of figures like the occultist Aleister Crowley (1875–1947) as well as Leland's *Aradia* (Taliesin 1965b: 19). Reflecting what is probably an influence from Ahmed's *The Black Art* and possibly also Shah's books, Taliesin nevertheless accepted the existence of a historical witches' religion, maintaining that this 'cult was undeniably of Saracenic origin', thus bearing 'little or no resemblance to the original Old Religion of these islands' (Taliesin 1965b: 19).

Joining Taliesin in attacking the Gardnerians through the pages of *Pentagram* was another esotericist, the London-born Roy Bowers (1931–1966), who used the pseudonym of Robert Cochrane. Like Taliesin, he claimed to come from a hereditary witch family, alleging that his great-grandfather had been 'the last Grand Master of the Staffordshire witches', and that, while this fact had been concealed from him as a child, he was later trained in witchcraft by his 'Aunt Lucy' (Cochrane 2002: 126, 151). Casting doubt on these claims were his widow and another family member, who – after his death – maintained that his claims on this front were untrue (Doyle White 2013: 84–5). He may have been involved in forms of modern religious witchcraft from the late 1950s, before establishing his own group, the Clan of Tubal Cain, in the early 1960s. This he led as its 'Magister', a Latin term for 'master', until his premature death in 1966 (Oates 2016; see also the alternative arguments in John of Monmouth 2012).

Accounts of this group by those who knew Cochrane and attended his rituals suggest a religion with certain similarities to Gardnerian Wicca. Valiente (1989: 117–18), for instance, described them worshipping 'the Goddess and the God as the ancient powers of primordial nature' and observing 'the Sabbats and the Esbats' on the same dates as the Gardnerians. However, Cochrane's private

---

[1] Taliesin reported that he disliked the term 'witch' (Taliesin 1965b: 18), although in his writing he nevertheless used 'witchcraft' and 'Craft' to describe his tradition. Robert Cochrane displayed a similar attitude to this terminology.

writings suggest a different personal approach. He referred repeatedly to 'the Gods' in the plural (Cochrane 1964: 8; 1965: 13), outlining a tripartite theology incorporating a Goddess, a God, and the Horn Child (Glass 1965: 142–6; Jones with Clifton 1997: 159–60). More broadly, Cochrane focussed primarily on a mystical pursuit of 'Truth' or 'Wisdom' and thus contact with 'Godhead' (Cochrane 1964: 8; 1965: 13). Key to this was the use of riddles and verses, often drawn from folklore or medieval literature, through which he believed that 'poetic inference' helped cultivate mystical illumination (Cochrane 2002: 27, 61). A clear influence here was the English poet Robert Graves (1895–1985), and especially the latter's 1948 work *The White Goddess* (Graves 1948), which Cochrane called 'that very excellent book' (Cochrane 2002: 176).

Cochrane emphasised the idea that witchcraft was the survival of the ancient 'Mysteries' (Cochrane 1965: 8; 2002: 50) and unlike the Gardnerians he sought to distinguish witchcraft as something apart from 'paganism', by which he meant 'religious pantheism' (Cochrane 2002: 82). Like Taliesin, he suggested that European witchcraft had absorbed Middle Eastern influences, arguing that around the time of the First Crusade, Persians bearing knowledge of the ancient Greek 'mystery tradition' had fled Islam and arrived in Britain and Ireland. Here, he maintained, their new ideas were absorbed by surviving druidic and bardic orders, resulting in the horned god becoming dominant within the witches' religion – a development that led to the previously tolerant Church initiating the witch trials to stamp it out (Cochrane 1964: 8; 2002: 59, 151). The likes of Gardner thus made a mistake in regarding witchcraft as 'the relics of a fertility religion' (Cochrane 2002: 69), Cochrane thought, and he went so far as to claim that Gardner had invented his tradition whole-cloth (Cochrane 2002: 23, 151).

What is clear is that, by leaning on an interpretation of witchcraft history coloured by Summers, Ahmed, and Shah, rather than that of Murray and Gardner, modern witches like Taliesin and Cochrane were able to set themselves and their traditions apart from Gardnerian Wicca and other Wiccan traditions that claimed to be the inheritors of an ancient European pre-Christian religion. Their typical tactic was to insist that Gardner had simply made up his religion, but that they instead represented genuine continuity with long-standing witchcraft traditions. Groups deliberately presenting themselves as 'traditional' witches continued to coexist alongside the Gardnerian and Alexandrian Wiccans during the 1970s and 1980s, receiving brief mention by writers like Stewart Farrar (1971: 4). However, it was only in the 1990s that this form of self-presentation grew rapidly within esoteric circles – a trajectory which has continued into the early decades of the twenty-first century. In many cases this new self-presentation was more rhetorical than substantive;

Hutton noted three covens that were founded as 'Wiccan' during the 1980s but began calling themselves traditional witches in the following decade (Hutton 2019: 399).

As argued elsewhere (Doyle White 2018a: 202–4), the growing popularity of the 'traditional witchcraft' label was probably influenced by two key factors that undermined the appeal of Wicca as a self-designation. The first was the growing association of the term 'Wicca' with a New Age–influenced, white-light aesthetic in the writings of Wiccans like the American Scott Cunningham (1956–1993), which undoubtedly put off those who favoured the more transgressive and darker connotations associated with witchery. The second factor was the growing criticism of the traditional Gardnerian origin story, primarily by the American Wiccan Aidan Kelly (b. 1940). If, as Kelly (1991) argued, Gardnerian Wicca was largely Gardner's own creation, then the term 'Wicca' would lose some of its connotations of ancient authenticity.[2] For many esotericists, the term 'traditional witchcraft' – or a synonym such as 'Old Craft' – was simply more appealing, providing a rhetorical evocation of an older world of rustic witchery.

Moreover, growing awareness regarding the flaws of the Murrayite interpretation resulted in many occultists placing renewed emphasis on the cunning folk as a lineage through which esoteric teachings could have been transmitted into recent periods (Cornish 2005: 365). This interest in the cunning folk among modern religious witches goes back at least to the 1960s; Cochrane, for example, referred to himself as a 'pellar' (Cochrane 2002: 28, 148), a Cornish synonym for a cunning person. More broadly, the terms 'cunning wo/man' were embraced as a self-designation by various practitioners in the traditional witchcraft milieu during the 1990s (Jackson 1996: 150; Fitzgerald and Chumbley 2011: 101; see also the very broad use of this term by Powell 2017). However, this late twentieth- and early twenty-first century use of the term 'cunning folk' differed from the ways in which the term has been employed by historians. Owen Davies, the foremost scholar of English and Welsh cunning folk traditions, has argued that, although there are areas of commonality between the historical cunning folk and some contemporary magical practitioners, the latter rarely provide unbewitching services, which was at the heart of what many cunning folk did, and moreover are rarely Christian, as their historical counterparts were (Davies 2003: 194–6). Nevertheless, by invoking links with the cunning folk, certain modern esotericists can circumvent the problem posed by historical arguments that organised witch groups never existed prior to the

---

[2] Ironically, Gardner never called his religion 'Wicca'. Instead, he referred to its practitioners collectively as 'the Wica' – an important distinction to make. The use of 'Wicca' as the name of the religion gained traction in the 1960s, especially after Gardner's death, and by the 1990s was solidly associated with Gardner and his tradition (see Doyle White 2010).

twentieth century, while also laying claim to the romanticised image of traditional healers living in rural cottages – an image with considerable aesthetic appeal.

This attempt to link contemporary practices with the image of the old village cunning woman is perhaps nowhere clearer than in the writings of Rae Beth (b. 1951), an English Pagan who published the popular book *Hedge Witch: A Guide to Solitary Witchcraft* in 1990. Beth portrayed the 'hedge witch' as being 'rather like the old-time village wisewoman or wiseman: one who "knows" and worships the Goddess and her consort, the Horned God', who performs magical rituals for benevolent ends, and who celebrates eight seasonal Sabbats each year (Beth 1990: 7, 20). This theological and ritual framework is essentially Wicca as it was developed by Gardner and other Gardnerians during the 1950s, but in this work the word 'Wicca' is avoided and instead the teachings are presented as 'hedge witchcraft', part of 'the Old Religion' with its 'roots in our neolithic past' (Beth 1990: 12). Beth was not alone in basically promoting a form of eclectic Wicca under a different guise. Several other writers active in the 1990s, largely in Britain, presented forms of religious witchcraft involving a horned god/goddess theology that was in part Wiccan-derived but which they were at pains to portray as something different, usually a 'traditional witchcraft' (Jones 1990; Jackson 1994; Gwyn [Michael Howard] 1999).

Another prominent figure to embrace the identity of the cunning man within the traditional witchcraft milieu was Andrew D. Chumbley (1967–2004). Chumbley was an English esotericist from Essex who, in the role of Magister, led a small group known as the Cultus Sabbati from 1991 until his untimely death. Although his was never a mass movement, he exerted a broader influence through his writings, in particular a series of grimoires which he both wrote and illustrated. Like Gardner and Cochrane, Chumbley claimed that his tradition, the Sabbatic Craft, was not his own creation but something largely inherited from earlier witches, and thus part of 'the traditional English Witch Cult' (Chumbley 2010: 25). Specifically, he claimed to have been initiated into two small esoteric traditions from different parts of Britain – but even if this is the case, it is evident that Chumbley's Sabbatic Craft owed much to his wide reading and to his own synthesis and innovation (Doyle White 2019). Chumbley was operating at a time when witchcraft historiography had moved on considerably from Murray and other writers of the Romantic school, and so he did not seek to identify the origins of his tradition in the late medieval or early modern periods. Instead, Chumbley presented his Sabbatic tradition as a successor of secretive nineteenth-century lodges established by urban magicians and rural cunning folk; he added that these esoteric groups had embraced some of the imagery of early modern witchcraft, especially that of the witches' sabbath, during the 1890s (Chumbley 2014a: 18). Chumbley's claims on this front remain unproven, although not impossible, but whatever their historicity, for our present purposes they are significant in representing another example by which a modern religious witch has emphasised their legitimacy via the medium of tradition.

The witches' sabbath was a central element of Chumbley's Sabbatic Craft, although, unlike the interpretations advanced by the likes of Gardner, Chumbley did not portray this sabbath as a literal assembly of practitioners in the physical world. Instead, he located the sabbath on a non-material level, as a timeless space to which a witch's spirit could travel while they were in a hypnagogic state. At the sabbath, he believed, the witch could encounter and learn from the spirits of other witches as well as non-human entities (Elwing 2014). Reflecting his broad reading, Chumbley – who was working on a PhD in the history of religions at the time of his death – drew links between his understanding of the witches' sabbath and the work of several continental European historians who had proposed the existence of 'dream-shamanism' in parts of early modern Europe (Chumbley 2014b: 209).

The notion that various communities in early modern Europe held beliefs involving some form of spirit-journeying, and that these beliefs sometimes became entangled in witchcraft accusations, emerged largely from the research of the Italian historian Carlo Ginzburg (b. 1939). Around the start of the 1960s, Ginzburg had discovered documents in an Udine archive that recounted how, in late sixteenth-century Friuli, Church inquisitors had come upon individuals calling themselves the *benandanti*. These *benandanti* maintained that, on certain nights, their spirits left their sleeping bodies and travelled to a field; there, in the name of God, they did battle with the spirits of nefarious individuals, the *maladanti* or witches, to ensure the protection of the crops. The inquisitors did not know what to make of these claims, and repeatedly sought to link them with the notion of the nocturnal witches' sabbath, suggesting that the *benandanti* were in reality witches themselves. Ginzburg's findings were published in Italian as *I Benandanti* in 1966, with an English-language translation following as *The Night Battles* in 1983. Here, Ginzburg argued that the *benandanti* were a 'fertility cult' (Ginzburg 1983: xx) and suggested that their nocturnal journeys might be a mental re-enactment of rites that in centuries past had taken place in person (Ginzburg 1983: 24). Ginzburg later expanded on these ideas in his 1989 book *Storia notturna*, published in English the following year as *Ecstasies*. In this book, the historian drew widely on recorded folk beliefs from various parts of Europe, most involving journeying during dream states, to argue for the existence of 'folkloric roots' to the stereotype of the witches' sabbath (Ginzburg 1990: 11).

Ginzburg's approach found favour among various other continental European scholars. Over the coming decades, similar ideas about European visionary traditions persevering from pre-Christian centuries into the early modern period – traditions scholars often labelled 'shamanic' or 'shamanistic' – were outlined in the writings of Hans Peter Duerr (b. 1943), Éva Pócs (b. 1936), Gábor Klaniczay (b. 1950), Wolfgang Behringer (b. 1956), and the aforementioned Henningsen. American and British scholars generally avoided similar interpretations of the early modern evidence, with the notable (and comparatively late) exception of Emma Wilby (b. 1963). It was nevertheless the case that many other scholars of early modern witchcraft beliefs remained somewhat sceptical regarding these interpretations, questioning the utility of the term 'shamanism' in this context and the implied idea that early modern folk beliefs that seemed at odds with ecclesial teaching must be pre-Christian survivals. Ginzburg, for instance, saw his arguments come under sustained criticism, most notably from Willem de Blécourt (b. 1951), who commented that Ginzburg combined 'a keen eye for detail with sweeping conclusions' (de Blécourt 2007: 126).

Just as Murray's ideas, although failing to find much support among professional historians, had discovered a receptive audience among many esotericists, so Ginzburg and those continuing his interpretative framework have been warmly embraced by many modern religious witches, especially those identifying as adherents of traditional witchcraft. Chumbley, for instance, repeatedly cited Ginzburg's work in particular and may well have been influenced by it when developing his own ideas (Elwing 2014: 256–7). Elsewhere, one can see other modern religious witches whose practice was directly informed by Ginzburg's writing. The scholar Diane Purkiss (1996: 44), for example, encountered one witch who described her own astral 'night battles' with malevolent forces over the Twyford Down roadworks in England, a clear adoption of the ideas Ginzburg explored in *I Benandanti*.

Another traditional witch who shared many of Chumbley's ideas and with whom he was in contact, Nigel Aldcroft Jackson (b. 1963), also cited Ginzburg's *Ecstasies*, alongside Duerr's *Dreamtime* (Duerr 1985), as 'indispensable studies' upon which he 'relied considerably' (Jackson 1994: 8). Confusingly, although Ginzburg had never accepted Murray's belief that the early modern witches were members of an actual pre-Christian religion who met to worship a horned god (Ginzburg 1983: xiii), Jackson tried to blend the two scholars' competing ideas, maintaining that Murray had 'proved [her case] very clearly' (Jackson 1994: 7). He went on to follow Gardner in presenting witchcraft as an ancient religion devoted to both a horned god and a goddess (Jackson 1994: 3), a marked contrast to Murray's almost exclusive focus on the former as the witches' deity. Similar confusion can be seen in Grimassi's work, where he claimed that Ginzburg's research on the *benandanti* provided good evidence for the existence of a pre-Christian witches' religion devoted to a horned god and a goddess (Grimassi 2000: 16, 82–5, 223), something that was not in the slightest bit true. In cases like those of Jackson and Grimassi, it seems that esotericists have embraced Ginzburg's work without really understanding it, and certainly not its place within the broader historiography of early modern witchcraft.[3]

There are other modern religious witches whose approach to Ginzburg is more careful. The Australian Lee Morgan, one of the most prominent traditional witchcraft authors of the 2010s, also praised Ginzburg's work while simultaneously acknowledging that Murray has been 'largely discredited' (Morgan 2013: 3, 17). Morgan noted the broad interest in Ginzburg's work among traditional witches, something that is also evident in the online presence of those active within this milieu. The website of the Cultus Sabbati, the group established by Chumbley, for instance lists the writings of Ginzburg, Duerr, Pócs, Behringer, and Wilby in its recommended bibliography – but not those of Macfarlene, Thomas, Cohn, Kieckhefer and so on. Meanwhile, in 2020, a Twitter user active in this milieu tweeted: 'Move over Ronald Hutton. If you're at all in the pagan/occult scene and haven't read the research of Carlo Ginzburg, Emma Wilby, or Eva Pocs yet —it's time to catch up' (Bane Folk 2020). Again and again, we see these specific authors invoked at the expense of other scholars writing on early modern witchcraft, authors selected because their ideas about visionary spirit-journeying chime with the specific interests of many modern religious witches.

References to the writings of historians are not the only way in which traditional witches have drawn legitimacy through an appeal to the past. Another recurring trait is the use of mock-archaic language, a tactic that we also saw in use among the early Wiccans. Thus, traditional witches often make reference to the likes of 'Wicce-craeft' (Jackson 1994: 2) and 'the Arte Magical' (Chumbley 2014a: 21). There is also a recurring emphasis on rurality and particularly on the folklore involving supernatural beings inhabiting rural areas. Indeed, folklorist Catherine Tosenberger (in press) has observed that traditional witches engage in what her fellow folklorist Michael Dylan Foster has termed 'the folkloresque', meaning 'creative, often commercial products or

---

[3] This type of misreading reminds me of Per Faxneld's point about contemporary Satanists. Through his fieldwork among North American Satanists he found that many practitioners believed that Church of Satan founder Anton LaVey was '*literally* an inheritor of secret esoteric traditions', thus failing to appreciate that LaVey's descriptions of a historic Satanic lineage was intended as ironic (Faxneld 2013: 78, italics in original).

texts ... that give the impression to the consumer ... that they derive directly from existing folkloric traditions' (Foster 2016: 5). The traditional witchcraft coven Ros an Bucca, for instance, which was founded in Cornwall around 2000, envelops itself in folkloresque imagery despite its theological and ritual framework owing little to traditional Cornish lore (as noted by Semmens 2010). This is all part of traditional witchcraft's reliance on the past as a means of legitimating contemporary practices.

Moreover, in a manner very reminiscent of Gardner and the early Wiccans, there are many statements made by traditional witches that reveal their desire to trace the origins of their new religions far back into pre-Christian periods of European history. Tony Steele – an English esotericist who established a group called the Ordo Anno Mundi in 1985 (Doyle White 2021b: 145–55) – claimed that 'Traditional Craft' groups shared 'a common origin in the Megalithic Culture of the Late Stone Age and Bronze Age' (Steele 2001: 6). Writing about what she preferred to call the 'Old Ways', 'Old Religion', or 'Old Forest Craft', Veronica Cummer described her tradition as having origins in the time of 'the Old Forest, the great haunted woodlands which used to cover most of Europe' (Cummer 2008: 11). Online, a practitioner using the moniker EchoWitch (n.d.) claimed that 'Traditional Witchcraft to the best of our knowledge pre-dates almost all of the other known religions of the planet and dates back to the paleolithic [*sic*] period'. Once again, we can see the past invoked as legitimation.

Seeking Satan

While the darker connotations of witchcraft held appeal for many traditional witches, this imagery would be embraced more overtly by another group of new religionists, those who openly embraced the label of Satanist. Witches had largely been equated with Satanists in the early modern imagination, although by the nineteenth century the two tropes – that of witchcraft and that of Satanism – had to an extent begun to disentangle, for instance allowing claims of Satan worship to be directed at Freemasons (Introvigne 2016: 158–226). Fears of active Satanism in late nineteenth-century France would be further stoked by French novelist Joris-Karl Huysmans (1848–1907) in his 1891 novel *Là-Bas*, a work described by scholar of literature Robert Ziegler as 'the most notorious Satanic novel of the era' (Ziegler 2012: 2). Although there is no firm evidence that any Satanists were genuinely active in France at that time, it is not impossible (Introvigne 2016: 149–50), and some people undoubtedly believed that Huysman's novel reflected real events. It would only be in the early decades of the twentieth century that we have clear evidence of certain European occultists embracing the veneration of Satan, although these individuals – who included the Danish Ben Kadosh (1872–1936) and the Polish Stanisław Przybyszewski (1868–1927) – exerted little influence, even within the esoteric milieu (Introvigne 2016: 227–34).

The first major form of modern religious Satanism appeared in 1966, with the formation of the Church of Satan in San Francisco. Its founder, Anton LaVey, would go on to further publicise his ideas in a series of books, most notably the 1969 work *The Satanic Bible*. LaVey's new religion, which came to be called LaVeyan Satanism, is rarely presented in academic writing as a form of new religious witchcraft, despite the fact he explicitly referred to his female followers as witches and their male counterparts as warlocks (LaVey 2005: 111–12). Emphasising this identity to the public, in the Church's early years LaVey launched a 'Topless Witches Revue' at a North Beach nightclub (Dyrendal, Lewis, & Petersen 2016: 54), and later titled his 1971 book *The Compleat Witch*.[4] Diabolist imagery drawn from early modern stereotypes was also woven into his tradition, as with his emphasis on Walpurgisnacht and Halloween as the two main holidays after a person's own birthday (LaVey 2005: 96). LaVey nevertheless foregrounded the identity of the Satanist over that of the witch, presenting Satan not as a literal being but as a representation of 'a force of nature' (LaVey 2005: 62), namely 'the carnal, earthly, and mundane aspects of life' (LaVey 2005: 55). Satan thus became an ideal symbol for LaVey, one who reminded humans that they were 'just another animal' (LaVey 2005: 25) with the same basic desires as almost any other species. He subsequently outlined a series of rituals, presented to manipulate magic, to help ensure that his followers could fulfil their desires.

As the historian of religion Per Faxneld has demonstrated, LaVey was interested primarily in 'the psychological effects of tradition' (Faxneld 2013: 90), on how evoking the past created an atmosphere conducive to a successful ritual. He did not claim to be continuing an actual tradition directly transmitted from witches past, as the likes of Gardner, Cochrane, and Chumbley had done. In his writings he nevertheless made repeated reference to the past in order to highlight individuals whom he thought had lived a Satanic way of life. For LaVey, these past Satanists included the Italian artist-cum-scientist Leonardo da Vinci, the Russian mystic Grigori Rasputin, and the Greek arms dealer Basil Zaharoff (LaVey 1972: 32; 2005: 104). LaVey did not reserve the term 'Satanist' for those who actively venerated Satan but, as noted by Faxneld (2013: 83), seemed to deem someone a Satanist if they 'were successful and

---

[4] Later reprinted as *The Satanic Witch*.

at the same time challenged the status quo'. Here, LaVey was clearly trying to place himself within some form of (indirect) historical lineage.

Unlike the Wiccans, LaVey did not emphasise a connection between the victims of the early modern witch trials and his modern-day practitioners. In his view, the trials saw the churches target 'the senile, sexually promiscuous, feeble-minded, deformed, hysterical, and anyone who happened to be of non-Christian thought or background' (LaVey 1972: 31). Few of those killed were actual witches, he maintained, for 'most of the real witches were sleeping with the inquisitors', having used their powers to ensure their own safety (LaVey 2005: 111). Even if he was not keen on presenting the victims of the witch trials as Satanists, LaVey was nevertheless interested in other groups whom he thought may have actually worshipped Satan in some form. His attention was particularly drawn to the Yezidis, an ethno-religious community originating in Kurdistan who had also intrigued earlier occultists like Crowley (Churton 2012). In LaVey's view, they were 'a sect of Devil worshippers' (LaVey 2005: 43), a notion based ultimately on their veneration of the Peacock Angel. He went on to maintain that the Knights Templars were 'exposed to the dualistic concepts of the Yezidis in the Near East' (LaVey 1972: 55), an idea reminiscent of Ahmed's. Thus, for LaVey, the Templars developed 'one of the most significant rites of Satanism', expressing 'prideful, life-adoring principles' (LaVey 1972: 55) and using the 'symbol of Baphomet . . . to represent Satan' (LaVey 2005: 136). He therefore suggested that the medieval military-religious order were genuine Satanists and in some sense forerunners of his own Church. How serious LaVey was in making these claims is nevertheless debatable. Faxneld believes that LaVey's historical claims here were knowingly ironic and mischievous (Faxneld 2013: 78), and certainly LaVey himself thought that Summers' writing was largely tongue-in-cheek (LaVey 2005: 103), perhaps suggesting that he saw his own work in a similar vein.

From his rather cynical view of modern religious witchcraft traditions, Rose noted that 'as long as witch-minded people exist, the cult does not need actual continuity, but only a claim to continuity such as they are predisposed to believe' (Rose 1962: 199). Rose's point highlights the strong desire that modern religious witches typically have for a sense of connection with the past, a feeling that they represent a continuity in tradition. Often, this is done to conceal the reality that they are participants in new religions. Even for those who accept the recent origins of their traditions, there is still a desire to hearken back to the past, to link today's witches to Palaeolithic shamans or early modern cunning folk. In this way, the association that witchcraft has with the past is an integral aspect of the witch's appeal.

2 Liberation

The historian Brian P. Levack noted that, in the early modern imagination, 'the witch was the quintessential rebel' (Levack 2016: 60). Not only did witches engage in severe antisocial acts at the expense of their neighbours but they also entered a pact with the Devil, thus aligning themselves with the forces of preternatural evil. Even with the diabolist elements drifting from the stereotype of the witch in subsequent centuries, these sorcerers remained figures fundamentally at odds with normality.

It has long been recognised that adopting the identity of the witch in modern Western contexts is a countercultural act. Calling oneself a witch is not something that most people do, and indeed it is the sort of statement likely to induce derision and ridicule more than respect. However, it is the very countercultural value of this act that is so often key to its appeal. As noted by the historian of esotericism Wouter Hanegraaff, the witch provides 'a *positive antitype* which derives much of its symbolic force from its implicit criticism of dominant Judaeo-Christian and Enlightenment values'. Thus, in Hanegraaff's view, 'there is hardly a better way to express one's rejection of the values informing mainstream [Western] society than claiming the name of its traditional enemies' (Hanegraaff 2002: 304–5, italics in the original). A similar point was made by folklorist Sabina Magliocco during her research among American Wiccans. She noted that the adoption of the witch was part of Wicca's 'oppositional culture', with practitioners 'construct[ing] their identity in contrast to that of the dominant American culture' (Magliocco 2004: 185). Calling oneself a witch is a very clear way of saying that you are different from the mainstream.

In this respect, modern religious witchcraft traditions are examples of what the scholar of religion Bruce Lincoln termed 'religions of resistance', in that they reject the 'religion of the status quo in part or in toto' (Lincoln 2006: 82–3). Of course, within modern Western societies, the reasons for a religion adopting an anti-status quo, countercultural identity are varied. Some religious minorities that do so, like Traditionalist Catholics (Cuneo 1997) or Folkish Heathens (Doyle White 2017a), become countercultural because they see the mainstream culture around them as one of degeneracy, and seek a return to a purer, less decadent past. For others, a countercultural identity is embraced as a vehicle of liberation through which they seek to resist what they perceive as oppressive conditions endemic within the dominant culture. It is in this latter category that modern religious witches can typically be found.

This idea of witchcraft as liberation has a long pedigree. Although they did not identify as witches per se, the so-called Romantic Satanists of the eighteenth and nineteenth centuries – the likes of Percy Bysshe Shelley (1792–1822), Lord Byron (1788–1824), and William Blake (1757–1827) – often perceived Satan, the master of witches, as a heroic rebel standing up to the unjust arbitrary authority of God (van Luijk 2016: 114). This Romantic sentiment was a likely influence on Jules Michelet, who in his 1862 historical study of witchcraft portrayed early modern witches as rebels against a deeply oppressive medieval clergy and feudal system. Michelet emphasised the womanhood of most early modern witches, with Per Faxneld noting that Michelet's work was 'probably the single most influential text presenting a sort of feminist vision of witches' (Faxneld 2014: 278). It may be through Michelet's influence that this idea of witchcraft as a liberatory movement of the poor appeared in Leland's *Aradia or the Gospel of the Witches*. Here, it was claimed that the goddess Diana sent her daughter, Aradia, to Earth to teach witchcraft to the oppressed, so that they might poison the aristocracy and blight the crops of rich peasants (Leland 1899: 4). Echoing Michelet, Leland added his view that it was the 'monstrous abuses of tyranny of Church and State' which drove 'vast numbers of the discontented' into the rebellious witches' religion during the Middle Ages (Leland 1899: 104). Texts like those of Michelet and Leland reveal that by the dawn of the twentieth century there was already an established tradition of portraying witchcraft as a force for countercultural resistance.

By the second half of the twentieth century, certain members of communities that lacked political, economic, and/or cultural dominance adopted the witch as a symbol of opposition to their marginalisation. Not only did they feel a sense of kinship with the accused witches of the early modern period but many went on to actively self-identify as witches too. By embracing many of the historical trappings and associations of witchcraft, these individuals soon set about trying to challenge and subvert the dominant authorities, in the hope both of enriching their own lives and of creating a future where they and the marginalised community they represented might exert greater social and cultural control. In this way, modern religious witchcraft became a tool for liberation.

A Feminist Witchcraft

Although male witches have appeared throughout history, in the European cultural imagination the witch has most usually been female. Indeed, of the individuals killed amid the early modern witch trials, a clear majority were women. Moreover, some of the tracts encouraging the hunt for witches – most famously Jacob Sprenger and Heinrich Kramer's *Malleus Maleficarum* from the 1480s – were strongly misogynistic. Probably because of these factors, there has long been a feminist interest in witchcraft. An early example can be seen in the writings of the American first-wave feminist Matilda Joslyn Gage (1826–1898), who in her 1893 book *Woman, Church and State* maintained that nine million people, the vast majority women, were killed as witches in medieval and early modern Europe (Gage 1893: 247). While Gage acknowledged that witch hunts had also taken place in pre-Christian periods, she claimed that the hunts intensified during the Late Middle Ages in large part owing to a Christian belief in the 'greater sinfulness of women' (Gage 1893: 225), a claim reflecting her broader antipathy towards organised Christianity. Early feminist interest in witchcraft is also discernible in literature, perhaps most prominently in the 1926 novel *Lolly Willowes*, written by English novelist Sylvia Townsend Warner (1893–1978) (Townsend Warner 1926). In Warner's novel, a middle-aged woman breaks from expected social conventions and reaches an agreement with the Devil that she will become a witch. As well as its underpinning feminist sentiments, the work also contained lesbian undertones, portraying what literature historian Marion Gibson called 'a distinctly Sapphic wallowing in witchcraft' (Gibson 2018: 63). The work was both a critical and a commercial success in Britain and the United States (Faxneld 2014: 646–7), likely contributing to the broader dissemination of its themes in the Anglophone cultural imagination.

The witch again proved a figure of interest in the second wave of feminism during the late 1960s and 1970s. In New York in 1968, a group of socialist-oriented feminists formed an activist group called WITCH – originally an acronym for the Women's International Terrorist Conspiracy from Hell – through which they engaged in witchcraft-themed political stunts (Echols 1989: 76, 96–8). In 1973, the Americans Barbara Ehrenreich (1941–2022) and Deirdre English (b. 1948), both involved in the women's health movement, published an influential short book, *Witches, Midwives and Nurses*. Here they claimed that the 'great majority' of those accused of being witches had in fact been 'lay healers serving the peasant population' (Ehrenreich and English 2010: 31), and that these healers had been targeted in 'a ruling class campaign of terror' (Ehrenreich and English 2010: 33). In this way, their interpretation emphasised an explicitly left-wing reading of history.

The witch trials also attracted attention from American writers committed to radical feminism, that is, those feminists who emphasised women's sex and/or gender, rather than their class, as the main axis of their oppression. In her 1974 work *Woman Hating*, Andrea Dworkin (1946–2005), drawing heavily on Pennethorne Hughes (Dworkin 1974: 207), presented the Murrayite narrative of European witchcraft as the survival of a religion dedicated to a horned god (Dworkin 1974: 121, 141–9). Like Gage, she also regarded these witch women as having considerable knowledge of botanical medicine and of psychic phenomena (Dworkin 1974: 139–40).[5] She repeated the claim that nine million people had been executed as witches and emphasised that women represented the vast majority of these victims (Dworkin 1974: 130, 136), framing the persecutions as 'gynocide' (Dworkin 1974: 134). For Dworkin, the persecutions demonstrated 'the absolute primal terror that women, as carnal beings, hold for men' (Dworkin 1974: 136) while, like Gage, she also saw in them a Christian view that women represented the 'root of all evil' (Dworkin 1974: 138).

Following on from Dworkin was Mary Daly (1928–2010), who addressed the topic of witchcraft in her 1978 book *Gyn/Ecology: The Metaethics of Radical Feminism*. Daly was not especially interested in what witchcraft really had been like – she only offered support for Murray's ideas at the close of her chapter on the subject, almost as an afterthought (Daly 1978: 219–20). Instead, Daly was interested in what she called the 'European witchcraze' (Daly 1978: 179) or, following Gardner, 'the Burning Times' (Daly 1978: 16, 210). She saw this as an explicit attempt by men to suppress women; the trials were a conspiracy by a 'secret gynocidal fraternity' to target 'women living outside the control of the patriarchal family' (Daly 1978: 186) – why, otherwise, were the majority of accused witches spinsters and widows (Daly 1978: 184)? More specifically, she argued that the persecutors represented a 'rising [male] professional hierarchy' who felt threatened by the 'spiritual wisdom and healing' of many women (Daly 1978: 195). Unlike Dworkin, Daly paid attention to the work of academic historians of witchcraft like Hugh Trevor-Roper, H. C. Erik Midelfort, and Jeffrey Burton Russell, if only to chastise them for what she regarded as their misogyny (Daly 1978: 184–5, 191, 204–6). For her, these historians, like the witch hunters before them, were agents of the 'Sado-State' that was committed to 'the torture, dis-memberment [*sic*], and murder of deviant women' (Daly 1978: 185). In this way, Daly emphasised continuity between the early modern period and the present. Evidence that 'the Burning Times continue', she claimed, could be seen in the fact that much feminist literature struggled to find a publisher, was allowed to 'go out of print', or, when published, faced 'bad reviews' and 'poor publicity' (Daly 1978: 217).

Heavily reliant on limited source material, most notably the *Malleus Maleficarum*, these radical feminist interpretations were at odds with established historical understandings of the early modern witch hunts, but on the whole were ignored by professional historians (barring, for instance, Harley 1990: 20–1). More sustained academic engagement with these writings came in

---

[5] Gage does not appear in Dworkin's sources here, so it is possible that the latter drew on Gage's work via intermediate sources.

the 1990s through the work of historian Diane Purkiss, who critiqued them not only for their factual inaccuracies but also on explicitly feminist grounds. Purkiss, for example, maintained that 'the myth of the Burning Times is not politically helpful', especially given that it portrays women as nothing but 'helpless victims' and the female body as merely 'a site of torture and death' (Purkiss 1996: 17).

In tandem with the arguments presented by the likes of Daly and Dworkin – arguments that both embraced and extended the Murrayite interpretation of witchcraft history – the United States was also witnessing the emergence of explicitly feminist-oriented forms of Wicca. Of key importance here was Zsuzsanna Budapest (Zsuzsanna Mokcsay, b. 1940), a Hungarian who arrived in the United States after fleeing the Soviet occupation of her country. Budapest eventually settled in Los Angeles, where she became closely involved in feminist activism. In 1971 she established the Susan B. Anthony Coven Number 1, named after the famous American suffragist, and through which she promulgated a modern Pagan tradition that came to be known as Dianic Wicca. Although drawing on established Wiccan traditions like Gardnerianism, the Dianic current differed in having a theology focussed almost exclusively on the Goddess and in only permitting women entry into its covens (Eller 1993: 55–8). Budapest asserted the importance of her Dianic practitioners calling themselves witches rather than using other, 'safe words, new-ageish words that don't threaten anybody', adding: 'I like the word witch. That is the only word in the English language that denotes woman [*sic*] with spiritual power' (Budapest 1986: 8). She made the political nature of her tradition abundantly clear. 'As feminist witches', she wrote, we 'draw upon our ancient tradition of using our magic and psychic powers as tools and weapons in our liberation' (Budapest 1986: 49).

Feminist-oriented Pagan witchcraft gained further traction through the work of another American, Miriam Simos (b. 1951), who used the name Starhawk. Starhawk had had some involvement with Budapest but had also been initiated into the Feri or Fairy tradition of Victor (1917–2001) and Cora Anderson (1915–2008) during the 1970s. She used these varied teachings as the basis for Reclaiming, a collective of practitioners that emerged in California at the end of that decade.[6] In addition, Starhawk began writing, and it was for her

---

[6] Practitioners of the Feri and Reclaiming traditions typically avoid calling themselves Wiccans and prefer the term witch. This likely stems largely from certain claims, once common in the American Pagan scene, that 'Wicca' rightfully applies only to British Traditional Wicca (that is, the Gardnerian, Alexandrian, and Algard traditions, which trace their initiatory lineage back to Gardner). Nevertheless, prominent founding figures in both Feri and Reclaiming did refer to their traditions as Wicca and there are evident commonalities with other Wiccan traditions.

books that she became best known. Hutton has noted that the most significant of Starhawk's works, *The Spiral Dance*, first published in 1979, 'replaced [Gardner's] *Witchcraft Today* as the model text for would-be witches' (Hutton 2019: 359). In *The Spiral Dance*, Starhawk repeated old tropes from Gardner's day, as with the claim that witchcraft was 'perhaps the oldest religion extant in the West' (Starhawk 1979: 2), but combined this approach with a strong feminist sensibility committed to challenging patriarchal social structures. Where she differed from Budapest's Dianic approach was in promoting a theology that included male gods alongside the Goddess and that was also open to mixed-sex covens. While Starhawk also saw being a witch as a feminist statement, for her this was not something just for women:

> 'to reclaim the word "Witch" is to reclaim our right, as women, to be powerful; as men, to know the feminine within as divine. To be a witch is to identify with 9 million victims of bigotry and hatred and to take responsibility for shaping a world in which prejudice claims no more victims'. (Starhawk 1979: 7)

Feminist ideas about witchcraft soon emanated beyond the United States, for example being absorbed by receptive esotericists and feminists in Britain during the late 1970s and 1980s (as explored in Feraro 2020). The 1990s then saw considerable academic research directed towards these feminist-oriented forms of Wicca, with published case studies focussing on groups active in San Francisco (Salomonsen 2002), Los Angeles (Coleman 2009), London (Greenwood 2000), and New Zealand (Rountree 2004). Meanwhile, the 1990s also saw a growth in studies of early modern witchcraft and its reception from academic historians informed by feminist theory (for instance Whitney 1995; Purkiss 1996; Gasser 2017). These writings were often critical of the factual distortions found in earlier radical feminist writings on witchery, but nevertheless recognised that witchcraft historiography had long been heavily male-dominated and had overlooked some of the gendered components to early modern witch hunting.

As highlighted by both journalistic (for instance Quaglia 2019; Lipscomb 2021) and academic (Corcoran 2022: 163) observers, the witch's role as a feminist icon underwent something of a resurgence amid the fourth wave of feminism that emerged in Western countries during the mid-2010s. An early sign of this was the re-creation of the WITCH group by Chicago-based activists in 2015, swiftly followed by subsequent branches forming in Portland and Boston the following year (Bess 2017). This revived interest could also be seen in the uptake of popular feminist books dealing with witchcraft, often reflecting developments in feminist theory, like intersectionality and sex positivity, that had gained traction since the writings of Daly and Dworkin (for instance Sollée 2017; Dickens and Torok 2021). This resurgence is perhaps also evident even in commercial branding decisions, as with The CW Network's declaration that their reboot of the witch-themed television series *Charmed* in 2018 was to be an explicitly feminist one (Goldberg 2018).

Queering Witchery

Women are not the only historically marginalised group within Western society to have been attracted by witchcraft. Accompanying the growing feminist interest in Wicca and witchcraft during the 1970s, various gay men in the United States also began to explore the identity of the witch. Associations between homosexuality and witchcraft were extant in Western culture by at least the late nineteenth century and were articulated by writers both sympathetic and hostile to same-sex sexual relations. In the former camp, the influential British homosexual writer Edward Carpenter (1844–1929) suggested that 'wizards' and 'witches' in many parts of the world were same-sex attracted (Carpenter 1914: 36–9), part of his broader argument about a 'world-wide attribution of magic powers to homosexuals' (Carpenter 1914: 47). Elsewhere, more negative assessments could also be found. In his 1891 novel *Là-Bas*, Huysmans derogatorily portrayed couplings between males at a Parisian Black Mass (Huysmans 2001: 228). These diabolist associations perhaps contributed to Gerald Gardner's view that gay men could not practise Wicca, a view maintained by some later Gardnerian Wiccans (Bourne 1998: 38–9). The Wicca established by these individuals employed a symbolically heterosexual framework, emphasising a male–female gender polarity as being necessary for working magic, something that was most visible in the Great Rite – an act of heterosexual sex magic (on sex magic see Urban 2005).

Many gay women and men were nevertheless attracted to Wicca. The prominent English Wiccan Alex Sanders was bisexual and initiated gay and bisexual men into his tradition (Di Fiosa 2010). Doreen Valiente, one of Gardner's high priestesses, later queried the exclusion of gay people from Wicca (Valiente 1989: 183), an attitude similar to that of her friend, the prominent English Wiccan Janet Farrar, who initiated 'many' homosexuals over the years (Farrar and Bone 2012: 25). Moreover, sociological studies indicate that, in the United States at least, the Wiccan and broader modern Pagan community has contained a notable minority of gay and bisexual practitioners (Orion 1995: 62; Berger, Leach, and Shaffer 2003: 28, 93). Many of these gay and bisexual people were clearly content to join established Wiccan traditions that operated around a heterosexual symbolic framework, but others adopted a different approach, forging variants that put same-sex attraction front and centre.

The most prominent of these groups was the Minoan Brotherhood. Its American founder, the New Yorker Eddie Buczynski (1947–1989), had been initiated into a Wiccan tradition known as the New England Covens of Traditionalist Witches in 1972 and then into the Gardnerian tradition the following year. The year 1972 had also seen him fashion his own Wiccan tradition, the Traditionalist Gwyddoniaid, which drew heavily upon medieval Welsh legend. Buczynski was gay, and by the latter half of the 1970s was interested in the idea of a Wiccan tradition explicitly catering to gay and bisexual men. In 1977 he founded the Knossos Grove, the first coven of the Minoan Brotherhood, a tradition for male-attracted men in which the inherited Wiccan framework was fleshed out with imagery from Minoan Crete (on Buczynski's life see Lloyd 2012; on the Brotherhood more broadly see Burns 2017 and Tully 2017). With his assistance, two of Buczynski's lesbian friends, Ria and Carol Bulzone, then established a variant for gay and bisexual women, the Minoan Sisterhood, in 1978 (Lloyd 2012: 418–20). Although the Minoan Brotherhood declined substantially in the 1990s, the vacancy it left was filled by other groups catering to gay and bisexual men, such as the Green Men, a Wiccan group formed in Boston in 1998 (Ford 2005: 1–2).[7]

Much as we have seen with the interaction between witchcraft and second-wave feminism, these practical religious developments were accompanied by intellectual considerations. This primarily took the form of a 1978 book, *Witchcraft and the Gay Counterculture*, written by the American gay liberation activist Arthur Evans (1942–2011). Providing a broad overview of European and American history, Evans' book was highly politicised and culminated in a condemnation of both capitalism and Marxist socialism alongside a call for 'a post-industrial communist nature-society where Gay culture can flourish free from repression and exploitation' (Evans 1978: 155). As part of its narrative, the book promoted the Wiccan-derived idea that Stone Age societies had been devoted to a mother goddess and a horned god, but added to this the concept that these ancient religions had held a special place for gay men, a notion reminiscent of Carpenter's arguments. Repeatedly citing the work of Margaret Murray, Evans adopted the idea that early modern witchcraft represented 'remnant [practices] of broken-down

---

[7] Other forms of modern Paganism also focussed on gay and bisexual men while not embracing the identity of the witch. The Temple of Priapus was established in Montreal in 1979, devoted to the adoration of the phallus and taking its name from that of an ancient Greek deity (Hays 2018). By the start of the twenty-first century, various Pagans were independently worshipping Antinous – the deified male favourite (and probable lover) of the Roman Emperor Hadrian – and subsequently formed into several groups (Doyle White 2016b; Doyle White 2017b). Although the Antinous worshippers do not consider themselves witches per se, some of them have had a prior involvement in Wicca (Doyle White 2016b: 39, 43).

strains of the old paganism' (Evans 1978: 77); however, in contrast to other writers of a similar vein, he stressed that 'male homosexuality and witchcraft were often linked together', believing that 'professional historians' had typically overlooked this because of their homophobic prejudices (Evans 1978: 75–6).

The identity of the witch also proved of interest to various transgender individuals. Probably the most high-profile transperson to declare themselves a witch was Anohni (b. 1971), the English-born but largely US-raised singer-songwriter. On her 2012 live album *Cut the World*, Anohni tells her audience that she is a witch – 'I actually de-baptised myself' – before adding that transgender people have a 'natural religion . . . you're almost automatically a witch. None of the patriarchal monotheisms will have you' ('Future Feminism'). Anohni proceeded to describe how she was raised Roman Catholic but later came to embrace the idea of the Earth as a goddess ('Future Feminism') and elsewhere has described her 'animist approach' to the world (Friedlander 2016). These ideas echo those of older figures such as Starhawk, and Anohni has made reference to the Starhawk-influenced Pagan subculture active in California when she was growing up there in the 1980s (Friedlander 2016).

Another trans singer-songwriter to display an interest in witchcraft has been the American Justin Vivian Bond (b. 1963). In the 2010s, Bond was repeatedly quoted as self-identifying as a witch (McCormack 2015; Sessums 2019), as well as a Pagan (Sessums 2019), while their music has repeatedly alluded to esoteric topics like the Ascended Masters ('The New Economy') and Aleister Crowley ('Crowley à la Lee'). Bond was also a painter and had been painting watercolours of people's left eyes for years; following the election of US President Donald Trump (b. 1946) in 2016, they began referring to these as 'witch eyes'. As Bond explained: 'When I was a kid, my family went on road trips. We would stop at souvenir shops that sold "devil eyes," which were supposed to protect you from evil. So, basically, I painted my "witch eyes" for people who don't want their lives to be invaded by patriarchal oppression' (Fulcher 2020).

Here we see both Anohni and Bond articulating their identification with the witch as an expressly feminist statement within the context of a trans-inclusive feminism. Other transpeople were also attracted by the identity of the witch, an overlap that gained increased media attention from progressive-aligned outlets in the mid-2010s (Donovan 2015; L. Wallace 2017).[8] Subsequent years also

---

[8] For the sake of clarity, here, 'progressive' designates progressivism, a specific ideology that emphasises continual legislative and societal reform and which typically relies on an underlying social-evolutionary narrative about ongoing and inevitable social progress (being on 'the right side of history') towards an end goal ('social justice') that, in contrast to the ideals of certain other leftist ideologies like Marxism, is not necessarily post-capitalist, classless, or economically

saw the growing appearance of trans characters in witchcraft-themed fiction, as in the American Netflix series *Chilling Adventures of Sabrina* (2018–2020), the 2020 US film *The Craft: Legacy*, and the 2022 novel *Her Majesty's Royal Coven* by English writer Juno Dawson (b. 1981) (Dawson 2022). Once again, this reflects the synergy between new religious witches and their popular culture counterparts.

At the same time as it was appealing to some transpeople, the identity of the witch was also embraced by certain gender-critical feminists, a group that contests the transgender rights movement's conception of gender identity and typically argues that the reforms proposed by transgender rights activists undermine women's sex-based legal rights and protections. For gender-critical feminists, who, from the mid-2010s onwards have often faced opposition from both major LGBT+ organisations and progressive-aligned institutions, the witch represents a symbol of demonised and persecuted women – the role that many gender-critical feminists see themselves in.

Often, gender-critical feminist adoptions of the witch echo those of second-wave activists.[9] The Wales-based gender-critical company Wild Womyn Workshop, for instance, produced products bearing slogans like 'We Are the Witches – Back from the Dead', 'Trouble-Making Witch', and 'This Witch Doesn't Burn'. The company came to broader attention in 2020 after J. K. Rowling, the English author of the witchcraft-themed Harry Potter books and by far the world's most famous gender-critical feminist, tweeted an image of herself wearing one of their T-shirts bearing the latter slogan (Rowling 2020). Indeed, perhaps because of Rowling's associations with witchcraft, commentators discussing her views have repeatedly evoked the subject of witchery in their use of language. Those criticising the vitriol and threats directed at Rowling have denounced the 'witch hunt' against her (O'Neill 2019; O'Doherty 2020; Cunliffe 2022), while a 2023 podcast series featuring the author was titled *The Witch Trials of J. K. Rowling*. Elsewhere, at a 2022 awards ceremony, the English actor Emma Watson (b. 1990) – who played teenage witch Hermione Granger in the film adaptations of Rowling's novels – described herself as being 'here for *all* the witches', a phrase widely interpreted as an attempt to signal support for the transgender rights movement and distance herself from Rowling's gender-critical opinions.

---

egalitarian. In the 2010s and early 2020s (the period discussed here), Western progressivism has generally focussed primarily on socio-cultural reform influenced by the identity politics of Black, LGBT+, and feminist activist groups, taking a form often denigrated by its critics as 'woke politics'.

[9] This may derive from the strong influence that radical feminism, a key ideological current within the second-wave feminist movement, has exerted on gender-critical thought.

While this discourse was playing out in Western societies, similar discussions had also been taking place within Wiccan and broader Pagan circles throughout the 2010s (Mueller 2017: 251). The 2011 PantheaCon event, held in San Jose, California, for instance generated considerable debate in the American Pagan scene after transwomen were reportedly denied entry to a women's ritual held there (Hoff Kraemer 2010: 277–9; Mueller 2017: 256–7). Several long-standing Wiccan women, especially the prominent Dianic practitioners Zsuzsanna Budapest and Ruth Barrett (b. 1954), subsequently faced vocal criticism and social ostracism for their alignment with gender-critical feminism and their opposition to the participation of transwomen in certain women's rituals (Mueller 2017: 261–6). It was in this context that a gender-critical, lesbian-run group formed in Towson, Maryland – the Pussy Church of Modern Witchcraft (PCMW).[10] On receiving recognition as a religious organisation from the Internal Revenue Service in 2018, the group received some press attention (Reilly 2018). Their online presence fizzled out within a couple of years, although one member – who had a background in Dianic Wicca – claimed that the PCMW had wanted to use social media only to reach like-minded people, rather than as an end in itself (Ward 2018). Even though the Pussy Church may prove marginal within the Wiccan community, it is interesting that it chooses to use the term 'witchcraft' so prominently in its self-presentation. Thus can be seen the continuing use of the witch as an avowed feminist statement within a new religious context, one present in the contrasting visions of both gender-critical and trans-inclusive feminism.

An African Heritage

Attention must now be turned to a third group of religious practitioners for whom the witch has been embraced as a symbol of liberation. The African diasporic traditions are different from the other groups that have been discussed here. Rather than being new religious movements established by White people in modern Western societies, as Wicca and LaVeyan Satanism are, these religions formed through the experiences of enslaved Africans transported to the

---

[10] The framing of the Pussy Church as being lesbian run suggests that it forms part of what could be called the contemporary lesbian, gay, bisexual (LGB) movement, a diffuse collection of groups and individuals critical of the way in which the mainstream gay rights movement transformed into a broader lesbian, gay, bisexual, transgender plus (LGBT+) or queer rights movement during the early twenty-first century. Their central argument has been that the interests of homosexual and bisexual people are different, and sometimes at odds with, the interests of transgender, non-binary, asexual, intersex, and other groups that are typically included under the broader LGBT+ banner. The contemporary LGB movement is itself ideologically diverse, combining both gender-critical feminists and social conservatives; its critics accuse it of being motivated largely by prejudice towards transgender people.

Americas. These diasporic traditions drew heavily on the traditional religious systems of various ethnic groups in West and Central Africa, but adapted to the changed, creolized social contexts that enslaved people and their descendants found themselves in, namely through the incorporation of European-derived elements, mostly forms of Christianity but in places also ideas from ceremonial magic and Freemasonry.

The forms that these new religions took in the Americas varied. In areas where Protestantism was dominant, these African-influenced traditions often focussed on spell-casting and healing, as with the Obeah of the British West Indies and the Hoodoo or Conjure of the United States. Conversely, in Roman Catholic territories these traditions often emerged as more fully religious systems, replete with deity worship and communal celebrations, such as the Vodou of Haiti, the Santería of Cuba, and the Candomblé of Brazil. After arising among European Americans during the 1840s, Spiritualism also spread to African diasporic communities, often via the Spiritist tradition of the French writer Allan Kardec (1804–1869). In many parts of the Americas, Spiritualism syncretised with African-derived traditions to form new variants, which in Spanish-speaking areas became known as Espiritismo.[11]

African diasporic traditions were typically regarded negatively by the dominant European, Christian elites who ruled over these African populations. In many cases, these elites passed laws attempting to restrict African-derived traditions, a process that itself shaped such practices into the forms we recognise today. The European colonial elites usually viewed these African diasporic traditions through the conceptual frameworks and accompanying terminology that they had inherited from their European past. Thus, Eurocentric terms such as 'witchcraft' and 'magic' (both in English and in their cognate versions from the French, Spanish, and Portuguese languages) were used to characterise and describe these African-derived traditions.[12] Many of the earliest publications exploring these traditions readily adopted this sort of language, reflected in the likes of Hesketh Bell's 1889 book *Obeah: Witchcraft in the West Indies* (Bell 1970) or Fernando Ortiz Fernández's 1906 work on Santería, *Los negros brujos* [*The Black Witches*].

By at least the close of the twentieth century, some practitioners of African diasporic traditions had adopted these European-derived terms as a means of

---

[11] Such intersections of African diasporic communities and traditions with European-derived esotericisms are encompassed within the promising sub-field of 'Africana esoteric studies', a term coined by Stephen C. Finley, Margarita Simon Guillory, and Hugh R. Page, Jr. (Finley et al. 2015: xiii).

[12] As Yvonne Chireau has noted, the earliest accounts of Hoodoo were written by European Americans in the seventeenth century and typically labelled Hoodoo practitioners with English-derived terms like 'witch' and 'cunning men' (Chireau 2003: 20–1).

self-identification. In Cuba, for example, various practitioners of Palo, a religion informed heavily by BaKongo traditional practices, began to embrace the term *brujería* (witchcraft) for their tradition (Ochoa 2010: 1). Similarly, in Puerto Rico, various Espiritismo mediums more open to vernacular practices were also referring to their practices as *brujería* (Romberg 2003: x). The use of such terms in these contexts can be seen as a form of reappropriation, as marginalised groups took the negative terms thrown at them and embraced them as a means of self-definition.

There is thus a history of people practising African diasporic religions using the term 'witch', or cognate words from other European languages, to describe themselves. However, as has been noted by the scholar of religion Marcelitte Failla (2022: 30), the 2010s saw a visible growth in the number of Black people doing so, at least in the United States. There are probably multiple reasons for this, including a renewed emphasis on Black cultural pride encouraged by the Black Lives Matter movement, the proliferation of social media, and an increase in the portrayals of African-descended witches in US popular culture, as can be seen in *American Horror Story: Coven* (2013), the *Charmed* reboot (2018–2022), and *Juju: The Web Series* (2019).[13]

One of the most organised expressions of African diasporic-oriented religious witchcraft to emerge in the United States was a group established in 2016, the Dawtas of the Moon, which began running an annual Black Witch Convention in Baltimore, Maryland, that year. The group had been founded by Iya Omitola Yejide Ogunsina-Fowler, a practitioner of Ifá, a divinatory system associated primarily with the Yoruba people, but on its website it emphasised that it was open to Black women from a range of non-Christian religious traditions, whether 'Hoodoo, Witchcraft, ... the path of Shamanism', or 'Native American rootwork'. Although the Dawtas had used the word 'witch' prominently in the name of their annual event, they acknowledged that 'not everyone is fond of the word' and that they welcomed members who did not consider themselves witches (Dawtas of the Moon n.d.a, n.d.b). A similar embrace of the term 'Black witch' can be seen in the work of Lakeesha Harris, a Chicago-based practitioner of Santería. In 2015 she launched an online coven called Black Witch Chronicles and the following year set up Black Witch University, intended to offer online courses pertaining to African traditional and African diasporic religions,

---

[13] Black witches were nevertheless present, if in often less-prominent roles, in American popular media from at least the mid-1990s onward. One of the four witches in the 1996 film *The Craft* was played by Black actress Rachel True, while multiple Black witches appeared as one-off characters in the television series *Charmed* (1998–2006).

supplemented with several in-person meet-ups (Ramgopal 2016). Harris explained to an interviewer from *Vice* how, for her, this identity had a political dimension: 'Calling myself a Black witch is to understand the political nature and the power that title holds for me – as a woman and as a witch and as someone taking ownership of her magic and her whole body' (Ramgopal 2016).

While these groups were facilitating in-person events, press sources like *The Atlantic* (Samuel 2018) observed that most Black witches were largely interacting online, utilising social media channels like Facebook, Tumblr, TikTok, and Instagram. On the last of these channels, for instance, hashtags that emerged in reference to this milieu included the likes of #blackwitchesofinstagram and #blackbrujasofinstagram. These outlets could gather considerable followings. At TikTok, for example, Black witch-themed hashtags had collectively amassed 32 million views by 2022 (Failla 2022: 30).[14]

This online activity is interrelated with a broader, if largely White-dominated, digital subculture, one comprising young self-described witches who interact predominantly through social media platforms – perhaps most famously through the TikTok hashtag #WitchTok (on this see Orrell 2019; Miller 2022).[15] While there were clear similarities with the teen witchcraft trend of the late 1990s and early 2000s (Berger and Ezzy 2007; Johnston and Aloi 2007), namely through the age demographic involved and its commercialised nature, this development of the late 2010s and early 2020s differed in at least three key respects.[16] First, it was shaped predominantly by highly visual forms of social media, whereas the 1990s/2000s trend drew more on television, film, print material, and internet forums. Second, it was far more overtly performative, focussed heavily on instructional videos (especially on TikTok and YouTube) or

---

[14] There is a caveat here: while most of these posts seem to use Black as a marker of racial identity, it is apparent that some of those employing these hashtags are instead using 'black witchcraft' and/or 'black magic' in the sense of cursing or to reflect that they pursue a darker, Goth-influenced aesthetic.

[15] At the time of writing, Chris Miller (2022) has produced the most significant scholarship on this new digital subculture, although his characterisation of it as Pagan is likely a misunderstanding; there are certainly many Pagans involved in it, but other participants appear committed to non-Pagan traditions such as Hoodoo or the New Age. A more accurate description would be to consider this subculture (as a whole) within the concept of esotericism.

[16] It is probably a mistake to see the two trends – in the late 1990s/early 2000s and then the late 2010s/early 2020s – as wholly distinct phenomena. Teenagers and other young people continued to develop an interest in witchcraft in the intervening decade, if potentially in lower numbers, much as they had done before the 1990s. These peaks in youth interest in modern religious witchcraft have likely been fuelled in part by popular culture depictions, for instance with *Sabrina the Teenage Witch* (1996–2003), *Buffy the Vampire Slayer* (1997–2003) and *Charmed* (1998–2006) and then later the *Chilling Adventures of Sabrina* (2018–2020) and the *Charmed* reboot (2018–2022).

displays of altars and ritual practice (especially on Instagram).[17] Third, it was less obviously dominated by Wiccan models of religious witchcraft, with many practitioners apparently engaged in spell-casting, healing, and divination without a clear theological framework, or instead influenced largely by practices drawn from the New Age milieu or from Hoodoo.[18] It thus provided a space where different ritual and religious traditions could cross-pollinate, and this resulted in some Black Hoodoo practitioners expressing concern about what they regarded as the misappropriation of African-derived ritual practices by White witches, especially when the latter were using these practices for commercial gain (Bess 2015).[19]

The societal discourse about Black witches was increasingly evident in the spate of mainstream media coverage given to African diasporic spiritualities in the wake of Black Lives Matter, especially in progressive-aligned outlets. In many cases it is apparent that the individuals being referred to with this term are practitioners of African diasporic traditions from the continental United States. An article in *Vulture* commented that it employed 'black witches' as 'a catch-all term' for individuals 'including rootworkers and voodoo priestesses' (Bastién 2017), while *Variety* quoted the Los Angeles-based Hoodoo practitioner N'ganga Makhosi apparently referring to herself and others as Black witches too (Bell 2020). This broad use of the word 'witch' can also be seen in books from this period. In their 2021 feminist work *Missing Witches*, the Canadian writers Risa Dickens and Amy Torok accompanied biographical accounts of self-described (Pagan) witches like Valiente and Budapest with those of the Haitian Vodou manbo Mama Lola (1933–2020) and the American novelist Zora Neale Hurston (1891–1960), who had a particular interest in African diasporic traditions. As Dickens and Torok noted, they included women in their list who did not identify as witches, consciously using the term as a 'big tent' designation (Dickens and Torok 2021: 4). In *Missing Witches*, we can thus see the use of the

---

[17] This sometimes drew accusations within the online milieu that certain individuals were 'Instagram witches' or 'poser witches', persons more interested in displaying a witchy aesthetic than in actually practising witchcraft (Frampton and Grandison 2022: 16).

[18] We need a good etic term to characterise these self-described witches who draw eclectically on different influences without being obviously part of an established tradition such as Wicca or Hoodoo. I might suggest 'eclectic religious witchcraft', although admittedly that term is not very catchy.

[19] The role of commercial activities within the WitchTok community warrants further investigation. The use of ritual practices as a means of earning money (whether through divination, creating amulets, offering healing remedies, etc.) is long-standing and can be found in many parts of the world, including in both European cunning traditions and most African diasporic religions. It was also evident in Wiccan-influenced forms of witchcraft from at least the late twentieth century, with the sociologist Douglas Ezzy observing that 'Witchcraft has colonised and utilised consumer capitalism for its own ends and consumerist capitalism has colonised contemporary Witchcraft for it[s] ends' (Ezzy 2006: 16).

third definition of the witch that was laid out in the introduction to this Element, the notion of the witch as an independent woman.

In practice, within these social milieus the term 'witch' was becoming a label for almost any woman (and also a few men) engaged in supernaturally oriented ritual or religious traditions outside the main Abrahamic faiths. Accompanying its growing use among practitioners of African-derived spiritualities, 'witch' could for instance also be seen increasingly used for vernacular ritual specialists of Mexican background (Rasbold 2020; Ruelas 2022). Sometimes, the word was even used to encompass elements of Christianity itself. *Vice* interviewed a New York-based Black witch who expressed the view that 'Catholicism is extremely witchy . . . it is witchcraft, they just don't want to call it that' (VICE Life 2021).

Associations of witchcraft with Black identity, especially in the United States, also appeared through music during the 2010s. The American rapper Azealia Banks (b. 1991) attracted international media attention in 2016, for instance, after she described herself as a practitioner of 'brujería', by which she meant Palo, while revealing evidence of animal sacrifices she had performed in a closet (Pérez 2021; see also initial media responses, such as Crucchiola 2016; Quinn 2016). That same year, another American rapper, Princess Nokia (b. 1992), released a song titled 'Brujas' in which she described herself as a 'ghetto witch' and emphasised her Yoruba ancestry. The song's music video, directed by the rapper with Asli Baykal, began with praise songs to the West African orisha Yemaja before re-enacting scenes from influential 1996 film *The Craft*, albeit with an entirely Black cast, reflecting the influence both of African diasporic religion and of pop culture portrayals of witchcraft. The term 'Wiccan', as opposed to 'witch', was also being utilised in a similar manner. In 2013, the Jamaican-American rapper Zebra Katz (b. 1987) released 'BLK WICCAN', ostensibly a song about sexual attraction but which also drew on terminology associated with witchcraft and Paganism ('potion', 'heathen', etc.). The song's video, created by Mara Zampariolo, featured a range of dancers, several evidently from gay or queer subcultures, perhaps a reference to Katz's own self-described queer identity and which may reflect the value of the witch identity as a statement of minority sexual orientation.

Unsurprisingly, many White occultists involved in forms of European-oriented modern religious witchcraft have also taken a practical interest in African diasporic traditions. Andrew Chumbley, for instance, attended a drumming group in London that was reportedly informed by Haitian Vodou, while his successor as Magister of the Cultus Sabbati, the American Daniel Schulke, also had some background in Afro-Caribbean practices (Doyle White 2019: 199, 208). Another public advocate of traditional witchcraft, the

Norwegian Nicholaj de Mattos Frisvold (b. 1970) – who had been associated with both Chumbley's Cultus Sabbati and Shani Oates' Clan of Tubal Cain – relocated to Brazil in 2003 and published books on the African diasporic traditions of Obeah, Palo, Quimbanda, and Ifá. The prominent English Wiccans Janet Farrar and her husband Gavin Bone also travelled to the Americas during the early decades of the twenty-first century and there encountered practitioners of Santería and Vodou, subsequently drawing on African diasporic ideas about trance possession in their publications (Doyle White 2021c). That largely White, Western esotericists should take an interest in religious traditions from other parts of the world should come as no surprise. Similar situations have been documented repeatedly by scholars, from New Age appropriations of Native North American traditions (Aldred 2000) through to various occultists' embrace of the skeletal Mexican folk saint Santa Muerte (Hedenborg White and Gregorius 2017).

While some practitioners of African diasporic traditions, often living in Western countries, were beginning to make use of the term 'witch' as a means of self-description, in many parts of Africa the situation was very different. As in much of the Americas, European colonial occupation of Africa resulted in European terminologies and categories being imported and imposed on indigenous populations. On the African continent, terms like 'witchcraft' and 'magic' were again used to interpret traditional indigenous concepts, including by anthropologists, most famously in E. E. Evans-Pritchard's influential 1937 work *Witchcraft, Oracles and Magic Among the Azande* (Evans-Pritchard 1937). Over time, various African communities adopted the English-language term 'witchcraft' to describe their own concepts of supernatural malevolence. This has gone hand-in-hand with new witch hunts across postcolonial African societies, which, in seeming contrast with earlier hunts, have often targeted children as alleged witches (La Fontaine 2016: 75–80).

There is therefore a juxtaposition between the trajectories of the terms 'witch' and 'witchcraft' between Africa and Western nations. In the latter, the period since 1900 has seen these terms increasingly purged of their negative valence and used in a positive sense to describe benevolent wielders of supernatural power. In Africa, meanwhile, these terms have come to be increasingly common but almost always with more traditional, and highly negative, connotations. There is one country in particular where these two meanings have found themselves in conflict: South Africa, home to the largest European diaspora on the African continent. Here, there has been a growing community of Wiccans since the 1990s, primarily drawn from the White South African minority, who self-identify as witches. At the same time, many of the country's Black ethnic groups understand a witch to be a person who performs malevolent acts.

This has resulted in some discord between South African Pagans and traditional healers active in the country, the latter calling for a negative definition of witchcraft to be enshrined in law (D. Wallace 2012, 2017).

Here, we have seen how part of the appeal of the witch is the figure's associations with the marginalised, the countercultural, and the rebellious. While historic European conceptions of the witch consistently framed her rebellious nature as being linked to her intrinsic malevolence, the broadening of the term 'witch' to encompass non-malicious wielders of supernatural power has allowed this aspect of the witch to appeal to more and more people. While feminist women were probably the earliest to embrace the witch's potential as an icon of liberation, they were soon followed by gay and bisexual people and then by transgender individuals and members of the African diaspora. There is no reason to assume that the adoption of the witch will stop there, with it being possible that modern religious witchcraft will gain traction in other communities in decades to come.

3 Power

Elliot Rose observed that in the early modern world 'the witch ... was distinguished from her neighbours by her claims to secret sources of power' (Rose 1962: 219). This idea, that the witch is a figure possessing abilities not available to most ordinary people, is one that has echoed through the centuries. One can trace these ideas as far back as ancient Greece. In Homer's *Odyssey*, the figure of Circe – who is a minor goddess rather than a witch, but who contributed to later European stereotypes of witchery – is capable of turning men into pigs. By the early modern period, witches were being accused of raising storms, hexing livestock, and flying through the air. After the witch trials had largely ended, notions of witches performing amazing feats continued to circulate in folklore, literature, and, later on, film and television.

In *The Devil Rides Out*, Dennis Wheatley's 1934 tale of diabolism in modern Britain, the character of Tanith – who accepts that she is a witch, even if she finds that a 'stupid old-fashioned term' – reveals that she first embarked on her occult studies 'to gain power – real power over other people's lives and destinies' (Wheatley 1970: 85). Similarly, in the 2016 American film *The Love Witch*, the Wiccan protagonist Elaine comments that 'people always ask me why I'm a witch. I tell them it's because I want to have magical power. But it's not like it sounds. All it is is using your will to get what you want.' These quotations are from fictional characters, but they nevertheless offer insight into a third key reason why modern-day people have chosen to embrace the witch. Although witches, or at least accused witches, have often become victims in

European history, at the same time they represent figures who are widely regarded as having powers that are simply not available to the majority of people. As various scholars have already recognised (for instance Greenwood 2000: 135; Pearson 2002: 163), the notion that witches are fundamentally powerful is key to why many individuals would want to become one.

The Allure of Magic

Throughout European history, the power of the witch has often come from their spell-casting – their knowledge of particular rituals through which they can manipulate the fabric of reality, usually to cause harm to their enemies. While we can certainly find instances in which spell-casting (or something that looks a lot like it) has been employed by recognised religious authorities, in European history the practice has generally been considered to belong not to the category of religion but to another, less salubrious category of behaviour, that of magic.

While 'witchcraft' certainly has been a contested term, one given various competing definitions, the word 'magic' has been even more confused. Today, 'magic' can be used in the English language to mean a range of different things, with very little to connect them. 'Magic' can describe the manipulation of the physical universe through supernatural power, especially in fantasy fiction; it can refer to the illusionism of 'magicians' who employ sleights of hand to entertain audiences; or it can describe something as being aesthetically special or enjoyable – 'it was a magical evening', for example.

The term 'magic' has long played a role in European history, for much of which it has been positioned in a duality against which to define either religion or science (Smith 2004: 215). In some cases it has instead been seen as a third category, straddling the border between the religion–science dichotomy (Josephson-Storm 2017: 15). In general, it has been a category into which European and Western people have simply dumped any ritual activities or supernaturally oriented beliefs that they did not think fitted into their preconceived notion of what religion should be, and has thus encompassed a broad range of practices from forms of healing and divination through to astrology and cursing. The term originated in the ancient Iranian word *maguš*, which was adopted by the ancient Greeks in the late sixth and early fifth centuries BCE. Among the Greeks, it bore connotations of foreign, dangerous, and fraudulent rites (Otto and Stausberg 2014: 16). After Christianity became dominant in Europe, the term 'magic' was retained, and continued to be used to define certain beliefs and practices as being set apart from Christian religion. This, in turn, could result in differences of opinion. Various Protestants, for instance, accused the Roman Catholics of engaging in magic rather than proper religion as a result of their highly ritualised approach to worship (Styers 2004: 37). 'Magic', like 'paganism' and 'superstition', was essentially a pejorative, stigmatising term.

By the nineteenth century, various scholars were adopting the term 'magic' and giving it their own definitions, hoping to use it as a tool of academic analysis. An influential example was the English anthropologist Edward Tylor (1832–1917), who presented magic as a worldview based on mistaken connections between things that were, in reality, 'mere analogy or symbolism' (Tylor 1903: 117). In Tylor's view, magic was dominant in 'the lowest known stages of civilization' but had also remained as a 'survival' in societies that had reached higher stages of development (Tylor 1903: 112–13). Tylor's approach was built upon by the Scottish anthropologist James Frazer (1854–1941), who also presented magic as a worldview resulting from 'misapplications of the association of ideas' (Frazer 1922: 12), one rooted in false belief in invisible connections between different things. He presented magic as being the earliest intellectual phase in humanity's development, one that was superseded by religion – by which he meant the propitiation of deities – and then, ultimately, by science (Frazer 1922: 711). As the scholar of religion Randall Styers has noted, scholars of this period often defined magic in such a way as to make it a 'definitive characteristic of the "primitive" mentality' and thus it became 'an important ideological tool' of European colonialism and imperialism (Styers 2004: 14). In this approach, magic was something found among far-off hunter-gatherers or gullible European peasants, and was deemed intrinsically inferior to the worldview of the rationalist upper-class European male.

In recent decades some astute observers, primarily operating within the history of religion, have concluded that the word 'magic' is best rejected altogether as an etic term of scholarly enquiry. As they have noted, because magic was a particular (largely derogatory) category within the history of Western thought, its use as a term for comparing different beliefs and practices of widely varying origin is just not helpful. The well-known scholar of religion Jonathan Z. Smith declared that he could 'see little merit in continuing the use of the substantive term "magic" in second-order, theoretical, academic discourse. We have better and more precise scholarly taxa for each of the phenomena commonly denoted by "magic" which, among other benefits, create more useful categories for comparison' (Smith 2004: 218). Like later commentators Bernd-Christian Otto and Michael Stausberg (Otto and Stausberg 2014: 11), Smith emphasised that scholars can use terms like 'healing', 'divination', 'amuletic', and 'cursing' quite readily without any need to turn towards the problematic overarching label of magic (Smith 2004: 218). This approach appears to have gained some acceptance within the academic study of esotericism, reflected for instance in the perspective of Wouter Hanegraaff, who proclaimed that 'the term "magic" is an important object *of* historical research, but definitely unsuitable as an etic instrument *for* doing research. It should simply not be used as a general category' (Hanegraaff 2012: 168, italics in original). This is a coherent and serious argument, and one that warrants much greater attention throughout the humanities and social sciences.[20]

However, as Hanegraaff's comment makes clear, even if 'magic' is an inappropriate term for scholars to use in a cross-cultural, etic manner, we still need to be aware of the important role that the term and the attendant concept have played in European and Western history. Indeed, because of the way that the term has helped to categorise practices and beliefs, for centuries there have been people performing rituals, typically invoking supernatural forces, that they actually call 'magic'. Many of these individuals have even labelled themselves 'magicians'. They have embraced practices often stigmatised by their own societies, and in doing so have adopted an oppositional stance with parallels to the countercultural approach of modern religious witches.

To encompass these practices, Otto (2016) devised the etic label 'Western learned magic'. He used this term to categorise 'a *continuous* and *coherent* textual and ritual "tradition"' (Otto 2016: 164, italics in original) stretching from the ancient world to the present day, transmitted from texts like the late ancient *Papyri Graecae Magicae* through to the early modern grimoires and thence to more recent esoteric traditions such as Thelema and Wicca. Intriguingly, he also saw fit to describe this Western learned magic as a 'religious' tradition, at least as religion is often understood from the perspective of modern scholarship on the subject (Otto 2016: 166).

Although there is a rhetorical transmission from the ancient world to the present, actual definitions as to what this magic is, and what it has incorporated, have varied considerably. As Otto noted, 'the semantics of "magic" change so substantially that one can hardly speak of a homogenous concept of "magic"— or a stable ritual art—that would have been shared by its practitioners from

---

[20] To my knowledge, the argument that 'magic' is a wholly inappropriate etic term for academic analysis has never been *successfully* refuted. The argument has, unfortunately, often been ignored, especially by scholars working in fields outside the study of religion who are simply unaware of it. Thus, the term 'magic' continues to appear in an etic sense in the work of many historians, folklorists, archaeologists, and anthropologists, who often use it without giving even a stipulative definition of what they mean by it. This persistence in the etic use of 'magic', like the continuing etic use of similarly inappropriate terms like 'shamanism', likely owes much to a lack of interest in theoretical and terminological issues among many scholars, the emotional attraction that the term holds for many people, and an awareness that the term appeals to the book-buying and museum-going public.

antiquity to today' (Otto 2016: 174). Many of those who practised rituals they regarded as magical in the medieval and early modern periods were unlikely to have understood these practices as being apart from the Christian (or in some cases Jewish) worldview that surrounded them. Such rituals often, for example, sought to invoke, and sometimes control, demons and angels, entities taken from a broadly Jewish and/or Christian cosmos.

Since at least the nineteenth century, efforts have been made to define this magic in the context of Enlightenment thinking. Hanegraaff noted that the twentieth century saw a 'dominant tendency' for self-described magicians to 'psychologize magic', highlighting for instance how various occultists espoused the idea that 'magical techniques are actually psychological techniques intended to develop a mystical consciousness' (Hanegraaff 2003: 366). In this way, many twentieth- and twenty-first-century magicians – in which category we should include most modern religious witches – were actually offering interpretations of magical rituals that differed in important ways from those of their predecessors. This reflected the fact that they were no longer operating in a world where Christianity was intellectually hegemonic but in one where science had largely replaced Christian religion as the arena typically believed to offer true insight into the world. The appeal to science as a legitimation strategy has, of course, been identified repeatedly among new religions (see, for instance, Hammer 2001; Lewis 2003: 14; Bigliardi 2023), although it has tended not to be overtly foregrounded in most forms of modern religious witchcraft.

By far the most influential definition of magic offered by a modern esotericist was that provided by Aleister Crowley. Born to a wealthy family, Crowley trained in Western learned magic as a member of the Hermetic Order of the Golden Dawn, one of the most influential esoteric groups in modern history. On breaking from the Order, he went on to pursue his interest in esoteric ideas and established the new religion of Thelema on the basis of a spiritual revelation purportedly received in 1904. Crowley later promoted the Thelemite religion through his leadership of an esoteric group, the Ordo Templi Orientis (OTO), as well as through his many writings (on Crowley see Sutin 2000; Kaczynski 2010). Crowley never self-identified as a witch, but in the final year of his life he had some contact with Gerald Gardner, with many of his ideas influencing Wicca and other forms of modern religious witchcraft (Bogdan 2009; Hutton 2012).

Crowley defined 'Magick' as 'the Science and Art of causing Change to occur in conformity with Will' (Crowley 1929: xvi). While Crowley's notion of Will had very specific connotations within his Thelemic system, the emphasis on will – as more commonly understood in general parlance – has also been emphasised in the approaches to magic evident among modern religious witches. Indeed, the scholar of religion Henrik Bogdan noted that Crowley's definition of magic(k) was 'arguably the best known' within modern esotericism and has influenced many other occultists (Bogdan 2012: 11). For Anton LaVey, magic was 'the change in situations or events in accordance with one's will, which would, using normally accepted methods, be unchangeable' (LaVey 2005: 110). According to Starhawk, magic is 'the art of changing consciousness at will' (Starhawk 1987: 79), reflecting the psychological interpretation highlighted by Hanegraaff. We can also see this emphasis on willpower in Gardner's statement that 'the *emotional factor*' was imperative in ensuring that spell-casting worked (Gardner 1954: 138–9, italics in the original), or similarly in the view of one of his high priestesses, Lois Bourne (1928–2017), when she commented that it is 'the amount of emotional energy' generated during a rite that will determine its success or failure (Bourne 1985: 105). This notion – that spells work because of the practitioner's willpower or emotional input, rather than the abilities of an invoked supernatural entity – is what makes the magic of most modern religious witches different from that of many earlier practitioners of Western learned magic.

These ideas are also regularly tied into the notion that magic operates through the manipulation of cosmic forces, energies, or powers as yet not understood by the scientific establishment. Thus, Gardner related that 'the essence of magic is usually to raise power, then to use or control it' (Gardner 1954: 101), later adding that 'the great art of using this Power would seem to be to believe firmly that you can do it and to have the fierce determination to make it work' (Gardner 1954: 153). Later Wiccans promoted similar ideas; the popular American practitioner Scott Cunningham could characterise magic as 'the projection of natural energies to produce needed effects' (Cunningham 1997: 19). Others sought to draw connections between the Wiccan understanding of magic and concepts found elsewhere in the world. Starhawk (1987: 100), for instance, linked the 'magical concept of energy' to the East Asian notion of *qi* and the Polynesian concept *mana*, while Doreen Valiente (1989: 94) speculated that this 'power' was the same phenomenon as the 'animal magnetism' of Franz Mesmer (1734–1815) and the 'orgone' of Wilhelm Reich (1897–1957). Non-Wiccan witches have emphasised similar ideas. Andrew Chumbley related that magic was 'a Universal Power', and its practice was 'concerned with the control of hidden energies via a complex cipher of Archetypes, Symbols and Correspondences' (Chumbley 2010: 19), while LaVey suggested that magical rites made use of 'bio-electrical energy' that could be generated through anger, terror, grief, or orgasm (LaVey 2005: 87–8). Here we can see an appeal to the language of science, albeit to describe concepts that would not be accepted by most mainstream scientists.

In a great many cases it seems that the spell-casting of Wiccans and other modern religious witches is intended to deal with life's pragmatic problems, often to do with health, relationships, and money worries. Bourne, for instance, related that 'much of the magical work' she undertook was 'trite and concerned with what most people would regard as the trivialities in people's lives', quite often encompassing 'lovelife and marital problems' (Bourne 1985: 113–14). Another prominent figure in the British Gardnerian community, Patricia Crowther, noted that her Sheffield coven often performed 'magic for people who write to us. These are usually requests for a return to good health, during a prolonged illness' (Crowther 2002: 157). Elsewhere, modern religious witches have cast spells to assist in legal issues. One of Chumbley's associates, for instance, recalled him producing a talisman for them when they had to testify in court (Doyle White 2019: 209), while Zsuzsanna Budapest and her Dianic Wiccans cast a spell to assist a woman's custody battle against her husband (Budapest 1986: 31). Broader social causes have also regularly attracted the attention of Wiccans. Crowther, for example, noted that her coven regularly performed rites to assist animal welfare charities (Crowther 2002: 158). Specific disasters can similarly attract a magical response. The anthropologist Susan Greenwood reported a London-based coven performing a ritual to send healing to the Shetland Islands after a major oil spill there in 1993 (Greenwood 2000: 87–8), while in 2017 I observed another London coven sending healing energies to the Yezidi people following the genocide waged against them by the Islamic State group.[21]

Cursing or hexing, which has historically lain at the heart of the older concept of witchcraft, is also practised by many modern religious witches. In her publications, Budapest included instructions on how to curse rapists and described how she and her Dianic Wiccans had performed such a rite themselves (Budapest 1986: 31–2, 46–7). LaVey also encouraged the use of cursing against anyone who has 'unjustly wronged you . . . or those dear to you' (LaVey 2005: 89), while Chumbley offered to curse an individual whom he believed had harmed one of his associates (Doyle White 2019: 209). However, many other modern religious witches consider cursing to be fundamentally unethical. Many, although by no means all, Wiccan traditions emphasise an ethical tenet called the Wiccan Rede, which typically holds to the statement 'An' it harm none, do what you will' (Doyle White 2015). Many Wiccans combine this with

---

[21] This was a ritual that I was invited to attend as a form of participant–observation. It was not part of an ongoing ethnographic project.

a belief in a rule of threefold return, which maintains that whatever a person does in their life – good or bad – will come back to them with three times the intensity (Doyle White 2016a: 112). This has echoes of popular Western conceptions of karma which, in contrast to long-established Asian understandings of this concept, hold that a person will get their comeuppance in the life they are now leading, as opposed to in future lifetimes in the cycle of rebirth.

Trying to straddle these ethical borderlands, some modern religious witches have professed that it is acceptable to use a spell to 'bind' another person from doing harm. This is obviously conceived as restricting a person's free will and freedom to act, but at the same time it is distinguished from a harmful curse. Probably the most famous example of such a binding came in the wake of the 2016 US presidential election, won by Donald Trump on a right-wing populist platform. Many modern religious witches were appalled at the prospect of a Trump presidency and turned to binding rituals in an attempt to restrain him, coordinating their efforts on social media as part of a 'Magic Resistance'. Media attention was soon drawn, especially when the pop singer Lana Del Rey (b. 1985) revealed her involvement via Twitter. In response, other occultists with sympathies for Trump's agenda, spearheaded by the Nevada-based David Griffin and Leslie McQuade, enacted their own rites with the intent of protecting the president (Asprem 2020; Magliocco 2020).

While the magic wars over Trump attracted considerable attention, especially as they were performed in the age of social media, rituals performed for a political reason have long featured in modern religious witchcraft. Gardner claimed that the witches who initiated him, a group now often known as the New Forest Coven, performed a rite called 'Operation Cone of Power' in the midst of the Second World War. According to Gardner's account, the witches raised a 'Cone of Power' inside a 'Great Circle' and directed it towards Adolf Hitler with the message 'You cannot cross the Sea. You cannot cross the Sea. YOU CANNOT COME. YOU CANNOT COME' (Bracelin 1960: 167). While the historicity of this event is in question, it at least demonstrates that the idea of spell-casting with political intent was in circulation from the early years of the Wiccan movement.

Decades later, American Wiccans were also performing rituals for explicitly political ends. Budapest's Dianic Wiccans, for instance, cast a spell against the 1978 California Proposition 6, which proposed a ban on gay men and lesbians teaching in public schools (Budapest 1986: 32). The anthropologist Loretta Orion recounted a 1985 ritual performed by a Wiccan coven on Long Island that was intended to ensure a pro-choice victory in a referendum on abortion being held in Bristol, Connecticut (Orion 1995: 258–9). However, the Wiccan figure best known for political activism was Starhawk. As well as taking part in a range of left-wing activist movements, she also introduced ritual elements into her campaigns. In one example from 1983, she led a group of women imprisoned in the Santa Rita County Jail, California in a ritual to cleanse the space they were contained in (Starhawk 1987: 149). Reflecting the highly politicised approach that Starhawk took to witchcraft, she linked magic with what she called 'power-from-within'. In her words, 'the technology of power-from-within is magic, the art of changing consciousness, of shifting shapes and dimensions, of bending reality' (Starhawk 1987: 15). She regarded power-from-within, which she also called 'empowerment', as something which 'arises from our sense of connection, our bonding with other human beings, and with the environment' (Starhawk 1987: 10). For Starhawk, power-from-within was one of three forms of power. The other two were 'power-over', through which one person could dominate another, and 'power-with', through which an individual can gain influence among a gathering of equals (Starhawk 1987: 9). In Starhawk's view, modern Western society is characterised by 'power-over', whereby authorities are able to dominate others in a patriarchal and hierarchical structure – and this was something she wanted to challenge, embracing a form of radical egalitarianism.

In these varied examples, we can repeatedly see how modern religious witches turn to rituals they term 'magical' as a means of trying to exert power in their lives. In this sense, adopting the identity of the witch can be an empowering experience. While modern religious witchcraft traditions are certainly not the preserve of society's most marginalised and dispossessed – there is considerable evidence for many practitioners being highly educated, middle-class, and employed in professional roles (Doyle White 2016a: 169–70) – it is also apparent that such traditions do attract individuals who may not feel empowered in other aspects of their lives. In the preceding section we saw how groups that may be socially marginalised on the basis of their sex or gender identity, sexuality, or racial background have been drawn to the witch as a liberatory figure, but it has also been argued that forms of modern religious witchcraft hold particular appeal for victims of child abuse (Greenwood 2000: 137, 142). In this sense, the witch can offer people who may feel a sense of powerlessness the notion that they are capable of taking direct ritual action both to improve their own life and to help exert some level of control in an often troubling world.

Elitism and Secretism

Modern witchcraft traditions are not alone among new religions in claiming that their practitioners can access special powers that are not possessed by the population at large. Many New Agers believe that they have enhanced abilities as lightworkers or earth angels destined to aid the planet. Spiritualists are of the view that many people are mediums, capable of communicating with the spirits of the dead. Scientologists allege that through the auditing process they can reach the level of Clear and thus gain enhanced memory recall. Ideas of this kind regularly form part of the appeal of various culturally alternative spiritualities. However, the historical association between witchcraft and spell-casting has meant that the identity of the witch is almost ideally suited for those wishing to claim abilities that the majority of humanity evidently lacks.

Even if situated within an ideology that is broadly egalitarian, the suggestion that certain individuals can possess special powers inevitably constructs this community as some sort of elite. Indeed, the notion of modern religious witches as an elite group certainly recurs in the writings of various practitioners. Gardner, for instance, stated that: 'Witchcraft was, and is, not a cult for everybody. Unless you have an attraction towards the occult, a sense of wonder, a feeling that you can slip for a few minutes out of this world into the other world of faery, it is of no use to you' (Gardner 1954: 29). Starhawk similarly declared that 'Witchcraft is not a religion of masses – of any sort' (Starhawk 1979: 13), while Chumbley insisted that 'Magic is not for everyone, [*sic*] if it were then it would be a commonplace vulgarity' (Chumbley 2010: 20). The practice of magic, and the identity of the witch, are thus presented in a somewhat elitist fashion, with practitioners setting themselves apart from the majority of people in a way that is not fundamentally different from the tactics of the aforementioned New Agers, Spiritualists, or Scientologists.

It is not hard to see how this sense of being special, a member of some sort of elite, might hold appeal for people who feel that they lack recognition in other facets of their life. Chumbley, for instance, was a working-class man who, at the time of writing the article quoted above, was in his early twenties. Thinking of himself as part of an elite capable of manipulating etheric power may have held a definite appeal in that context. Gardner was a far wealthier individual, and by the 1950s he had retired in comfort, but it seems probable that he still craved social recognition; he styled himself 'doctor' despite not having a doctorate from a recognised university (Valiente 1989: 41–2), and claimed to be an anthropologist (Gardner 1954: 18) yet possessed no anthropological qualifica-tions. Perhaps Gardner's failure to gain acceptance as a scholar contributed to the appeal that being a witch held for him. Figures like Gardner, Starhawk, and Chumbley were clearly intellectually curious people, keen readers and writers, who nevertheless received little reward for their efforts from dominant institu-tions; it is not surprising that they may have been attracted to the idea of being part of an altogether different, more countercultural sort of elite. This would accord with Bruce Lincoln's observation that the leaders of religions of resistance tend to come from the 'marginal intelligentsia', figures who do not occupy professional positions within the dominant state and societal apparatus (Lincoln 2006: 84).

In many respects, this discourse about witches forming a special elite also draws on the notion of secretism, something defined by Paul Christopher Johnson in his consideration of Brazilian Candomblé as 'the active milling, polishing, and promotion of the reputation of secrets' (Johnson 2002: 3). Thus, secretism involves an individual or group letting other people know that they possess secrets, but not then revealing what those secrets are, thereby cultivating an aura of mystery around themselves, adding to their potential allure. One of the foremost scholars of modern Paganism, Chas S. Clifton, first observed how secretism was a strategy often employed in modern religious witchcraft, both by Wiccans and by self-described traditional witches (Clifton 2006: 124; 2019: 240). Gardner wrote that on his initiation in 1939 he 'took the usual oaths of secrecy which bound me not to reveal any secrets of the cult' (Gardner 1954: 18). It is certainly possible that Gardner was telling the truth here, and that he was restricted by oaths or bonds of friendship with other modern witches, but the fact that he was publicly declaring that he held secrets which he could not share was nevertheless a clear case of secretism. Robert Cochrane similarly informed the journalist Justine Glass that while he could tell her certain things, he could not go 'into any great detail since the nature of my oath forbids it' (Glass 1965: 142). Chumbley wrote that he was privy to 'insider' lore from secretive British witch traditions that could not be disclosed to outsiders, and that he could thus only 'whisper in the wings of academic discourse that there is much more to the story of modern witchcraft than meets the eye' (Chumbley 2014a: 21). Again, this is secretism. In each case, the practitioner is not remaining silent but is communicating to a broader audience that they are the possessor of various secrets, the nature of which they then hint at in a manner that cultivates their own personal mystique.

While the discourse of elitism can be seen to play a small role in the writings of various aforementioned witches, it becomes especially evident in LaVey's work. Here, a perception of his followers as a religious elite was combined with a broader belief in the fundamental inequality of humanity, with certain individuals being intrinsically superior to others. This attitude stemmed from forms of right-wing libertarianism and Social Darwinism; the scholar of religion Amina Olander Lap (2013: 95) noted that influences on LaVey included the philosophers Herbert Spencer (1820–1903), Friedrich Nietzsche (1844–1900), and Ayn Rand (1905–1982). We can see this attitude in various passages from LaVey's writings, for instance his claim that it is 'the higher man's role to produce the children of the future. Quality is now more important than quantity'

(LaVey 1972: 12). Elsewhere, in *The Satanic Bible*, he quoted (without attribution) the 1896 book *Might Is Right* by Ragnar Redbeard: 'Death to the weakling, wealth to the strong!' (LaVey 2005: 30). For LaVey, the Satanist was a person willing to use their strength to dominate others, embrace their desires, and enhance their life.

We have seen how a third component of the witch's appeal lies in the figure's association with power. The image of the witch is intrinsically bound up with the notion of the spell-caster, the individual who can manipulate supernatural forces to bring about changes in the physical world – to heal, to help, or to hex. For modern people who may feel a sense of powerlessness, embracing the identity of the witch, and with it the practice of magic, can be a profoundly empowering act. Moreover, the witch also offers people an identity that is intrinsically selective; only a very small proportion of the population embrace such an identity in modern Western societies, rendering modern witches an elite of sorts. Their elitism may arise not from social status, economic advantage, or cultural influence but from a sense that they are fundamentally set apart from the majority through their power, an identity that they may reinforce through the practice of secretism. This too can be appealing for many people.

4 Conclusions

It would be simplistic to assume that there is any single reason, or even one clear set of reasons, why a person living in a modern Western society might choose to call themselves a witch and practise what they call witchcraft. A teenaged Australian boy who solitarily embraces LaVeyan Satanism is unlikely to be motivated by exactly the same factors as a thirty-year-old woman who joins a Dianic Wiccan coven in California. Everyone is different, with their own unique circumstances, experiences, and motivations. This Element has nevertheless sought to highlight three of the key overarching reasons as to why the witch remains a compelling image for those shaping their own self-identities in the modern world. It has highlighted the fact that witchcraft offers an image of continuity with the distant past, thus bringing a sense of authenticity to otherwise comparatively new religious and esoteric practices. It has considered how the witch's role as a countercultural figure set against the mainstream has provided inspiration for those seeing themselves as fighting for liberation from societal oppression. It has also demonstrated that witchcraft, being bound up with spell-casting, divination, and the vague concept of magic, can provide a sense of empowerment for those wishing to take charge in their lives.

Unable to foresee the future in a crystal ball, scholars of religion will be unable to say for sure how the witch will retain its popularity in future.

However, there is no reason to assume that the appeal of the witch will decline in the next century or so. Generations to come will no doubt still be attracted by the pull of tradition; there may well still be oppressed communities, in fact or in conviction; and people will still seek power over their lives, and sometimes also the lives of others. As long as these factors exist, the witch will retain some relevance. While contemporary witchcraft-oriented religious traditions like Wicca and LaVeyan Satanism will likely persevere – even if in smaller form than they exist today – it is also probable that new witchcraft religions will arise, adapting to changing social and cultural conditions. The twenty-first century has continued to show how new traditions can emerge that draw on the historical imagery of witchcraft while simultaneously finding new approaches to doing so. Whereas the Church of Satan discussed in this Element combines the identity of the Satanic witch with a right-wing libertarian philosophy, the 2010s saw the emergence of another American Satanist organisation that instead weds the traditional imagery of the Satanic witch with a left-wing, progressive ideology, the Temple of Satan (Laycock 2020, 2023). Thus, we can see how the same imagery and conceptual heritage can be embraced for new purposes.

In many Western countries, the emergence of increasingly ethnically and religiously heterogeneous populations may impact future uses of the terms 'witch' and 'witchcraft', offering new opportunities as well as new challenges. Migration, and in some cases also conversion, will probably see both African diasporic religions and African traditional religions gain a growing presence and visibility in many Western countries, especially in metropolitan urban areas. As discussed in Section 2, there are signs that some followers of these traditions are attracted to European-derived terms like 'witch' and 'bruja', and it is possible that these labels will be adopted by increasing numbers of those pursuing traditions like Palo, Hoodoo, and Espiritismo. At the same time, the growing presence of migrants from parts of the world where witchcraft is typically seen as a very dangerous and negative thing may generate further conflict with those who regard the witch as a positive, benevolent identity – a terminological clash we have already seen in South Africa (D. Wallace 2012, 2017).

There are other ways in which changing demographics will also pose challenges to those embracing the identity of the witch. While the number of Christians is clearly declining in Western countries, it is possible that specific interpretations of Christianity will gain a strengthened hold over particular communities or localities, at both the social and the governmental level – think, for instance, of the aims of so-called Christian Nationalism in the United States. Within these areas, claiming to be a witch may become increasingly risky. The popularity of QAnon conspiracy theories, and with them the claim that the US government is secretly run by a cabal of child-molesting

Satanists, demonstrates how paranoid fears influenced by earlier panics about witchcraft are still very much with us. It is by no means impossible that something akin to the Satanic ritual abuse hysteria of the 1980s and early 1990s could resurface in parts of the Western world. Indeed, it has been reported that in continental Europe and Latin America, where the panic arrived later, it persevered into the twenty-first century (Introvigne 2016: 456–7, 461). Growing ideological radicalisation and polarisation, the decline of good investigative journalism in the world of twenty-four-hour news cycles, and the spread of cancel culture and online harassment could all contribute to a situation that is hardly conducive to those proclaiming themselves a witch, at least in particular regions or social milieus.

There is thus some uncertainty about the future of modern religious witchcraft. On the one hand, the reasons why the witch has appealed to so many people will remain, and there will surely be individuals and groups who declare themselves witches in the decades and centuries to come. On the other hand, new threats and challenges will probably emerge, making the identity of the witch a risky one to embrace in certain places and at certain times. Observing how this situation develops will be of interest to scholars of new religions and alternative spiritualities as well as to all those who are fascinated by the complex role that witchcraft and the witch have played in the cultural history of the Western world.

References

Books and Articles

Ahmed, R. (1971 [1936]). *The Black Art*. London: Arrow Books.

Aldred, L. (2000). Plastic Shamans and Astroturf Sun Dances: New Age Commercialization of Native American Spirituality. *American Indian Quarterly*, *24*(3), 329–52.

Asprem, E. (2020). The Magical Theory of Politics: Memes, Magic, and the Enchantment of Social Forces in the American Magic War. *Nova Religio: The Journal of Alternative and Emergent Religions*, *23*(4), 15–42.

Bacigalupo, A. M. (2007). *Shamans of the Foye Tree: Gender, Power, and Healing Among Chilean Mapuche*. Austin, TX: University of Texas Press.

Baker, J. W. (1996). White Witches: Historic Fact and Romantic Fantasy. In J. R. Lewis, ed., *Magical Religion and Modern Witchcraft*. Albany, NY: State University of New York Press, 171–92.

Bane Folk (2020). [Twitter] 18 January. https://twitter.com/banefolk/status/1218669899838558208 (accessed 26 June 2023).

Baroja, J. C. (2001 [1964]). *The World of the Witches*. Translated by N. Glendinning. London: Phoenix Press.

Bastién, A. J. (2017). Why Can't Black Witches Get Some Respect in Popular Culture? *Vulture*, 31 October. https://bit.ly/3MQAj30 (accessed 26 June 2023).

Baum, L. F. (1900). *The Wonderful Wizard of Oz*. Chicago, IL: George M. Hill Company.

Bell, B. (2020). How Hollywood Has Failed Black Witches, According to Real Black Witches. *Variety*, 30 October. https://bit.ly/46nwZUj (accessed: 26 June 2023).

Bell, H. (1970 [1889]). *Obeah: Witchcraft in the West Indies*. Westport, CT: Negro Universities Press.

Berger, H. A., & Ezzy, D. (2007). *Teenage Witches: Magical Youth and the Search for the Self*. New Brunswick, NJ: Rutgers University Press.

Berger, H. A., Leach, E. A., & Shaffer, L. S. (2003). *Voices from the Pagan Census: A National Survey of Witches and Neo-Pagans in the United States*. Columbia, SC: University of South Carolina Press.

Bess, G. (2015). Black Magic: Hoodoo Witches Speak Out on the Appropriation of Their Craft. *Vice*, 23 September. https://bit.ly/47gKian (accessed 26 June 2023).

Bess, G. (2017). How the Socialist Feminists of WITCH Use Magic to Fight Capitalism. *Vice*, 2 October. https://bit.ly/3um4tVH (accessed 26 June 2023).

Beth, R. (1990). *Hedge Witch: A Guide to Solitary Witchcraft*. London: Robert Hale.

Bigliardi, S. (2023). *New Religious Movements and Science*. Cambridge: Cambridge University Press.

Black, M. (2020). *A Demon-Haunted Land: Witches, Wonder Doctors, and the Ghosts of the Past in Post-WWII Germany*. New York: Metropolitan Books.

Bogdan, H. (2009). The Influence of Aleister Crowley on Gerald Gardner and the Early Witchcraft Movement. In J. R. Lewis and M. Pizza, eds., *Handbook of Contemporary Paganism*. Leiden: Brill, 81–107.

Bogdan, H. (2012). Introduction: Modern Western Magic. *Aries: Journal for the Study of Western Esotericism*, *12*(1), 1–16.

Bourne, L. (1985 [1979]). *Witch Amongst Us: The Autobiography of a Witch*. London: Robert Hale.

Bourne, L. (1998). *Dancing With Witches*. London: Robert Hale.

Bracelin, J. L. (1960). *Gerald Gardner: Witch*. London: Octagon Press.

Budapest, Z. (1986). *The Holy Book of Women's Mysteries: Volume 1*. Rev. ed. Oakland, CA: Susan B. Anthony Coven No. 1.

Burns, B. E. (2017). Cretomania and Neo-Paganism: The Great Mother Goddess and Gay Male Identity in the Minoan Brotherhood. In N. Momigliano and A. Farnoux, eds., *Cretomania: Modern Desires for the Minoan Past*. London: Routledge, 157–72.

Burton, M. (2016 [1930]). *The Secret of High Eldersham*. London: British Library.

Carpenter, E. (1914). *Intermediate Types Among Primitive Folk*. London: George Allen and Co.

Chireau, Y. P. (2003). *Black Magic: Religion and the African American Conjuring Tradition*. Berkeley: University of California Press.

Christie, A. (1990 [1961]). *The Pale Horse*. Glasgow: Fontana/Collins.

Chryssides, G. D. (2003). Scientific Creationism: A Study of the Raëlian Church. In C. Partridge, ed., *UFO Religions*. London: Routledge, 45–61.

Chumbley, A. D. (2010). *Opuscula Magica Volume I – Essays: Witchcraft and the Sabbatic Tradition*. Richmond Vista, CA: Three Hands Press.

Chumbley, A. D. (2014a). The Magic of History: Some Considerations. In M. Howard and D. Schulke, eds., *Hands of Apostasy: Essays on Traditional Witchcraft*. Richmond Vista, CA: Three Hands Press, 15–24.

Chumbley, A. D. (2014b). Origins and Rationales of Modern Witch Cults. In M. Howard and D. Schulke, eds., *Hands of Apostasy: Essays on Traditional Witchcraft*. Richmond Vista, CA: Three Hands Press, 201–9.

Churton, T. (2012). Aleister Crowley and the Yezidis. In H. Bogdan and M. P. Starr, eds., *Aleister Crowley and Western Esotericism*. Oxford: Oxford University Press, 181–207.

Clifton, C. S. (2006). *Her Hidden Children: The Rise of Wicca and Paganism in America*. Lanham, MD: AltaMira Press.

Clifton, C. S. (2019). Witches Still Fly: Or Do They? Traditional Witches, Wiccans, and Flying Ointment. In S. Feraro and E. Doyle White, eds., *Magic and Witchery in the Modern West: Celebrating the Twentieth Anniversary of 'The Triumph of the Moon'*. Cham: Palgrave Macmillan, 223–43.

Cochrane, R. (1964). The Craft Today. *Pentagram*, *2*, 8. www.thewica.co.uk/pentagram-magazine.

Cochrane, R. (1965). The Faith of the Wise. *Pentagram*, *4*, 13–14.

Cochrane, R. (2002). *The Robert Cochrane Letters: An Insight into Modern Traditional Witchcraft*. Milverton: Capall Bann.

Cohn, N. (1975). *Europe's Inner Demons: An Enquiry Inspired by the Great Witch-Hunt*. London: Heinemann for Sussex University Press.

Coleman, K. S. (2009). *Re-Riting Woman: Dianic Wicca and the Feminine Divine*. Lanham, MD: AltaMira Press.

Corcoran, M. (2022). *Teen Witches: Witchcraft and Adolescence in American Popular Culture*. Cardiff: University of Wales Press.

Cornish, H. (2005). Cunning Histories: Privileging Narratives in the Present. *History and Anthropology*, *16*(3), 363–76.

Cornish, H. (2009). Spelling Out History: Transforming Witchcraft Past and Present. *The Pomegranate: The International Journal of Pagan Studies*, *11*(1), 14–28.

Cowdell, P. (2022). Folklore as MacGuffin: British Folklore and Margaret Murray in a 1930 Crime Novel and Beyond. In M. Cheeseman and C. Hart, eds., *Folklore and Nation in Britain and Ireland*. New York: Routledge, 190–204.

Crowley, A. (1929). *Magick in Theory and Practice*. Paris: Privately published.

Crowther, P. (2002). *From Stagecraft to Witchcraft: The Early Years of a High Priestess*. Chieveley: Capall Bann.

Crucchiola, J. (2016). Azealia Banks Filmed Herself Cleaning a Closet She Claims to Have Performed Witchcraft Rituals in, and That's Not a Euphemism. *Vulture*, 30 December. https://bit.ly/3G6qGJS (accessed 26 June 2023).

Cummer, V. (2008). *Sorgitzak: Old Forest Craft*. Sunland, CA: Pendraig Publishing.

Cuneo, M. W. (1997). *The Smoke of Satan: Conservative and Traditionalist Dissent in Contemporary American Catholicism*. Oxford: Oxford University Press.

Cunliffe, R. (2022). It's Time for the Witch Hunt Against JK Rowling to End. *New Statesman*, 7 January. https://bit.ly/3uk0qsR (accessed 26 June 2023).

Cunningham, S. (1997 [1988]). *Wicca: A Guide for the Solitary Practitioner*. St Paul, MN: Llewellyn.

Daly, M. (1978). *Gyn/Ecology: The Metaethics of Radical Feminism*. Boston, MA: Beacon Press.

Daraul, A. (1961). *Secret Societies: Yesterday and Today*. London: Frederick Muller.

Davies, O. (2003). *Cunning-Folk: Popular Magic in English History*. London: Hambledon Continuum.

Davies, O. (2013). *America Bewitched: The Story of Witchcraft after Salem*. Oxford: Oxford University Press.

Dawson, J. (2022). *Her Majesty's Royal Coven*. London: HarperVoyager.

Dawtas of the Moon (n.d.a). Frequently Asked Questions. *Dawtas of the Moon*. https://dawtasofthemoon.com/f-a-q-membership-page (accessed 19 March 2023).

Dawtas of the Moon (n.d.b). About the Occult Mama. *Dawtas of the Moon*. https://dawtasofthemoon.com/the-occult-mama (accessed 19 March 2023).

de Blécourt, W. (2007). The Return of the Sabbat: Mental Archaeologies, Conjectural Histories or Political Mythologies? In J. Barry and O. Davies, eds., *Palgrave Advances in Witchcraft Historiography*. Basingstoke: Palgrave Macmillan, 125–45.

Dickens, R., & Torok, A. (2021). *Missing Witches: Recovering True Histories of Feminist Magic*. Berkeley, CA: North Atlantic Books.

Di Fiosa, J. (2010). *A Coin for the Ferryman: The Death and Life of Alex Sanders*. Boston, MA: Logios.

Doherty, B. (2020). From Decadent Diabolist to Roman Catholic Demonologist: Some Biographical Curiosities from Montague Summers' Black Folio. *Literature & Aesthetics*, *30*(2), 1–37.

Donovan, M. (2015). How Witchcraft Is Empowering Queer and Trans Young People. *Vice*, 14 August. https://bit.ly/3QCXfE0 (accessed 26 June 2023).

Doyle White, E. (2010). The Meaning of 'Wicca': A Study in Etymology, History and Pagan Politics. *The Pomegranate: The International Journal of Pagan Studies*, *12*(2), 185–207.

Doyle White, E. (2013). An Elusive Roebuck: Luciferianism and Paganism in Robert Cochrane's Witchcraft. *Correspondences: An Online Journal for the Academic Study of Western Esotericism*, *1*(1), 75–101.

Doyle White, E. (2014). Devil's Stones and Midnight Rites: Megaliths, Folklore, and Contemporary Pagan Witchcraft. *Folklore*, *125*(1), 60–79.

Doyle White, E. (2015). 'An' It Harm None, Do What Ye Will': A Historical Analysis of the Wiccan Rede. *Magic, Ritual, and Witchcraft, 10*(2), 142–71.

Doyle White, E. (2016a). *Wicca: History, Belief, and Community in Modern Pagan Witchcraft*. Eastbourne: Sussex Academic Press.

Doyle White, E. (2016b). The New Cultus of Antinous: Hadrian's Deified Lover and Contemporary Queer Paganism. *Nova Religio: The Journal of Alternative and Emergent Religions, 20*(1), 32–59.

Doyle White, E. (2017a). Northern Gods for Northern Folk: Racial Identity and Right-Wing Ideology Among Britain's Folkish Heathens. *Journal of Religion in Europe, 10*(3), 241–73.

Doyle White, E. (2017b). Archaeology, Historicity, and Homosexuality in the New Cultus of Antinous: Perceptions of the Past in a Contemporary Pagan Religion. *International Journal for the Study of New Religions, 8*(2), 237–59.

Doyle White, E. (2018a). The Creation of 'Traditional Witchcraft': Pagans, Luciferians, and the Quest for Esoteric Legitimacy. *Aries: Journal for the Study of Western Esotericism, 18*(2), 188–216.

Doyle White, E. (2018b). Between the Devil and the Old Gods: Exploring the Intersection between the Pagan and Satanic Milieus. *Alternative Spirituality and Religion Review, 9*(2), 141–64.

Doyle White, E. (2019). Navigating the Crooked Path: Andrew D. Chumbley and the Sabbatic Craft. In S. Feraro & E. Doyle White, eds., *Magic and Witchery in the Modern West: Celebrating the Twentieth Anniversary of Ronald Hutton's The Triumph of the Moon*. Cham: Palgrave Macmillan, 197–222.

Doyle White, E. (2021a). Drawing Down the Moon: From Classical Greece to Modern Wicca? In B.-C. Otto & D. Johannsen, eds., *Fictional Practice: Magic, Narration, and the Power of Imagination*. Leiden: Brill, 222–43.

Doyle White, E. (2021b). In Woden's Shadow: Anglo-Saxonism, Paganism, and Politics in Modern England. In K. Fugelso, ed., *Studies in Medievalism XXX: Politics and Medievalism (Studies) II*. Woodbridge: D. S. Brewer, 129–56.

Doyle White, E. (2021c). Janet Farrar. *World Religions and Spirituality Project*, 18 March. https://wrldrels.org/2021/03/16/janet-farrar/ (accessed 26 June 2023).

Doyle White, E., & Feraro, S. (2019). Twenty Years On: An Introduction. In S. Feraro & E. Doyle White, eds., *Magic and Witchery in the Modern West: Celebrating the Twentieth Anniversary of Ronald Hutton's The Triumph of the Moon*. Cham: Palgrave Macmillan, 1–19.

Duerr, H. P. (1985). *Dreamtime: Concerning the Boundary between Wilderness and Civilization*. Translated by F. Goodman. Oxford: Basil Blackwell.

Dworkin, A. (1974). *Woman Hating*. New York: E. P. Dutton.

Dyrendal, A., Lewis, J. R., & Petersen, J. A. (2016). *The Invention of Satanism*. New York: Oxford University Press.

Echols, A. (1989). *Daring to Be Bad: Radical Feminism in America 1967–1975*. Minneapolis, MN: University of Minnesota Press.

EchoWitch (n.d.). What Is Traditional Witchcraft? www.angelfire.com/wizard/lightforce/witch.html (accessed 26 June 2023).

Ehrenreich, B., & English, D. (2010). *Witches, Midwives and Nurses: A History of Women Healers*. 2nd ed. New York: Feminist Press at the City University of New York.

Eller, C. (1993). *Living in the Lap of the Goddess: The Feminist Spirituality Movement in America*. Boston, MA: Beacon Press.

Elwing, J. (2014). Where the Three Roads Meet: Sabbatic Witchcraft and Oneiric Praxis in the Writings of Andrew Chumbley. In M. Howard and D. Schulke, eds., *Hands of Apostasy: Essays on Traditional Witchcraft*. Richmond Vista, CA: Three Hands Press, 249–71.

Evans, A. (1978). *Witchcraft and the Gay Counterculture*. Boston, MA: Fag Rag Books.

Evans, D., & Green, D., eds. (2009). *Ten Years of Triumph of the Moon*. St Albans: Hidden Publishing.

Evans-Pritchard, E. E. (1937). *Witchcraft, Oracles and Magic among the Azande*. Oxford: Clarendon Press.

Ezzy, D. (2006). White Witches and Black Magic: Ethics and Consumerism in Contemporary Witchcraft. *Journal of Contemporary Religion*, *21*(1), 15–31.

Failla, M. (2022). Assembling an Africana Religious Orientation: The Black Witch, Digital Media, and Imagining a Black World of Being. *The Black Scholar*, *52*(3), 30–40.

Farrar, J., & Bone, G. (2012). Witchcraft and Sexuality: The Last Taboos. In S. Thompson, G. Pond, P. Tanner, C. Omphalos, & J. Polanshek, eds., *Gender and Transgender in Modern Paganism*. Cupertino, CA: Circle of Cerridwen Press, 25–8.

Farrar, S. (1971). *What Witches Do: A Modern Coven Revealed*. New York: Coward, McCann & Geoghegan.

Favret-Saada, J. (1980). *Deadly Words: Witchcraft in the Bocage*. Translated by C. Cullen. Cambridge: Cambridge University Press.

Faxneld, P. (2013). Secret Lineages and De Facto Satanists: Anton LaVey's Use of Esoteric Tradition. In E. Asprem & K. Granholm, eds., *Contemporary Esotericism*. Sheffield: Equinox, 72–90.

Faxneld, P. (2014). *Satanic Feminism: Lucifer as the Liberator of Woman in Nineteenth-Century Culture*. Stockholm: Molin and Sorgenfrei.

Feraro, S. (2020). *Women and Gender Issues in British Paganism, 1945–1990*. Cham: Palgrave Macmillan.

Feraro, S., & Doyle White, E., eds. (2019). *Magic and Witchery in the Modern West: Celebrating the Twentieth Anniversary of Ronald Hutton's The Triumph of the Moon*. Cham: Palgrave Macmillan.

Finley, S. C., Guillory, M. S., & Page Jr., H. R. (2015). Preface. In S. C. Finley, M. S. Guillory, and H. R. Page, Jr., eds. *Esotericism in African American Religious Experience: 'There Is a Mystery'*. Leiden: Brill, xii–xiii.

Fitzgerald, R., & Chumbley, A. D. (2011). The Sabbatic Cultus: An Interview with Andrew D. Chumbley. In A. D. Chumbley, ed. *Opuscula Magica Volume 2: Essays on Witchcraft and Crooked Path Sorcery*. Richmond Vista, CA: Three Hands Press, 101–17.

Ford, M. T. (2005). *The Path of the Green Man: Gay Men, Wicca, and Living a Magical Life*. New York: Citadel Press.

Foster, M. D. (2016). Introduction: The Challenge of the Folkloresque. In M. D. Foster and J. A. Tolbert, eds., *The Folkloresque: Reframing Folklore in a Popular Culture World*. Logan: Utah State University Press, 3–33.

Frampton, A., & Grandison, A. (2022). 'In the Broom Closet': Exploring the Role of Online Communities in Shaping the Identities of Contemporary Witchcraft Practitioners. *Current Psychology*, 1–21.

Frazer, J. (1922). *The Golden Bough: A Study in Magic and Religion*. Abridged ed. London: Macmillan and Co.

Friedlander, E. (2016). Anohni's Eyes Wide Open Campaign. *Vice*, 21 April. https://bit.ly/3N7WXEe (accessed 26 June 2023).

Fudge, T. A. (2006). Traditions and Trajectories in the Historiography of European Witch Hunting. *History Compass*, 4(3), 488–527.

Fulcher, S. E. (2020). Justin Vivian Bond: The Eyes Have It. *Provincetown Independent*, 27 August. https://bit.ly/3GnEJLq (accessed 26 June 2023).

Gage, M. J. (1893). *Woman, Church and State: A Historical Account of the Status of Woman Through the Christian Ages*. 2nd ed. New York: The Truth Seeker Company.

Gardner, G. (1954). *Witchcraft Today*. London: Rider and Company.

Gardner, G. (1971 [1959]). *The Meaning of Witchcraft*. London: Aquarian Press.

Gardner G. (1999 [1949]). *High Magic's Aid*. Louth: I. H. O. Books.

Gasser, E. (2017). *Vexed with Devils: Manhood and Witchcraft in Old and New England*. New York: New York University Press.

Gibson, M. (2018). *Rediscovering Renaissance Witchcraft*. London: Routledge.

Ginzburg, C. (1983). *The Night Battles: Witchcraft and Agrarian Cults in the Sixteenth and Seventeenth Centuries*. Translated by J. and A. Tedeschi. Baltimore, MD: Johns Hopkins University Press.

Ginzburg, C. (1990). *Ecstasies: Deciphering the Witches' Sabbath*. Translated by R. Rosenthal. London: Hutchinson Radius.

Glass, J. (1965). *Witchcraft, the Sixth Sense – and Us*. London: Neville Spearman.

Goldberg, L. (2018). 'Charmed' Star Rips CW's 'Feminist' Reboot: 'Guess We Forgot to Do That the First Go Around'. *The Hollywood Reporter*, 26 January. https://bit.ly/3N1ECsn (accessed 26 June 2023).

Graves, R. (1948). *The White Goddess: A Historical Grammar of Poetic Myth*. London: Hutchinson.

Greenwood, S. (2000). *Magic, Witchcraft and the Otherworld: An Anthropology*. Oxford: Berg.

Gregorius, F. (2013). Luciferian Witchcraft: At the Crossroads between Paganism and Satanism. In P. Faxneld & J. A. Petersen, eds., *The Devil's Party: Satanism in Modernity*. Oxford: Oxford University Press, 229–49.

Grimassi, R. (2000). *Italian Witchcraft: The Old Religion of Southern Europe*. 2nd ed. Woodbury, MN: Llewellyn.

Gwyn [M. Howard] (1999). *Light from the Shadows: A Mythos of Modern Traditional Witchcraft*. Chieveley: Capall Bann.

Hammer, O. (2001). *Claiming Knowledge: Strategies of Epistemology from Theosophy to the New Age*. Leiden: Brill.

Hanegraaff, W. J. (2002). From the Devil's Gateway to the Goddess Within: The Image of the Witch in Neopaganism. In J. Pearson, ed., *Belief Beyond Boundaries: Wicca, Celtic Spirituality and the New Age*. Aldershot: Ashgate, 295–312.

Hanegraaff, W. J. (2003). How Magic Survived the Disenchantment of the World. *Religion*, *33*(4), 357–80.

Hanegraaff, W. J. (2012). *Esotericism and the Academy: Rejected Knowledge in Western Culture*. Cambridge: Cambridge University Press.

Harley, D. (1990). Historians as Demonologists: The Myth of the Midwife-Witch. *Social History of Medicine*, *3*(1), 1–26.

Harrison, M. (1973). *The Roots of Witchcraft*. London: Frederick Muller.

Hays, M. (2018). Inside the Montreal Temple That Worships the Dick. *Vice*, 7 March. https://bit.ly/3T4HHMi (accessed 26 June 2023).

Hedenborg White, M. (2019). 'The Eyes of Goats and of Women': Femininity and the Post-Thelemic Witchcraft of Jack Parsons and Kenneth Grant. In S. Feraro & E. Doyle White, eds., *Magic and Witchery in the Modern West: Celebrating the Twentieth Anniversary of 'The Triumph of the Moon'*. Cham: Palgrave Macmillan, 175–96.

Hedenborg White, M., & Gregorius, F. (2017). The Scythe and the Pentagram: Santa Muerte from Folk Catholicism to Occultism. *Religions*, *8*(1), 1–14.

Hoff Kraemer, C. (2010). Conference Report: PantheaCon 2011. *The Pomegranate: The International Journal of Pagan Studies, 12*(2), 276–80.

Hughes, P. (1952). *Witchcraft*. London: Longmans, Green & Co.

Hutton, R. (1995). The Roots of Modern Paganism. In G. Harvey & C. Hardman, eds., *Paganism Today*. Hammersmith: Thorsons, 3–15.

Hutton, R. (1999). *The Triumph of the Moon: A History of Modern Pagan Witchcraft*. Oxford: Oxford University Press.

Hutton, R. (2003). *Witches, Druids and King Arthur*. London: Hambledon Continuum.

Hutton, R. (2010). Writing the History of Witchcraft: A Personal View. *The Pomegranate: The International Journal of Pagan Studies, 12*(2), 239–62.

Hutton, R. (2011). Revisionism and Counter-Revisionism in Pagan History. *The Pomegranate: The International Journal of Pagan Studies, 13*(2), 225–56.

Hutton, R. (2012). Crowley and Wicca. In H. Bogdan & M. P. Starr, eds., *Aleister Crowley and Western Esotericism*. Oxford: Oxford University Press, 285–306.

Hutton, R. (2017). *The Witch: A History of Fear, from Ancient Times to the Present*. New Haven, CT: Yale University Press.

Hutton, R. (2019). *The Triumph of the Moon: A History of Modern Pagan Witchcraft*. 2nd ed. Oxford: Oxford University Press.

Huysmans, J. K. (2001 [1981]). *The Damned (Là-Bas)*. Translated by T. Hale. London: Penguin.

Introvigne, M. (2016). *Satanism: A Social History*. Leiden: Brill.

Jackson, N. (1994). *Call of the Horned Piper*. Chieveley: Capall Bann.

Jackson, N. (1996). *Masks of Misrule: The Horned God and his Cult in Europe*. Chieveley: Capall Bann.

John of Monmouth (2012). *Genuine Witchcraft Is Explained: The Secret History of the Royal Windsor Coven and the Regency*. Milverton: Capall Bann.

Johnson, P. C. (2002). *Secrets, Gossip, and Gods: The Transformation of Brazilian Candomblé*. Oxford: Oxford University Press.

Johnston, H. E., & Aloi, P., eds. (2007). *The New Generation Witches: Teenage Witchcraft in Contemporary Culture*. Aldershot: Ashgate.

Jones, E. J. (1990). *Witchcraft: A Tradition Renewed*. London: Robert Hale.

Jones, E. J. with Clifton, C. S. (1997). *Sacred Mask, Sacred Dance*. St Paul, MN: Llewellyn.

Josephson-Storm, J. A. (2017). *The Myth of Disenchantment: Magic, Modernity, and the Birth of the Human Sciences*. Chicago, IL: University of Chicago Press.

Josiffe, C. (2014). British Voodoo: The Black Art of Rollo Ahmed. *Fortean Times, 316*, 28–34 and *317*, 42–7.

Kaczynski, R. (2010). *Perdurabo: The Life of Aleister Crowley.* Revised ed. Berkeley, CA: North Atlantic Books.

Kelly, A. A. (1991). *Crafting the Art of Magic: A History of Modern Pagan Witchcraft Volume I: 1939–1964.* St Paul, MN: Llewellyn.

La Fontaine, J. (2016). *Witches and Demons: A Comparative Perspective on Witchcraft and Satanism.* New York: Berghahn.

Lap, A. O. (2013). Categorizing Modern Satanism: An Analysis of LaVey's Early Writings. In P. Faxneld & J. A. Petersen, eds., *The Devil's Party: Satanism in Modernity.* Oxford: Oxford University Press, 83–102.

LaVey, A. S. (1972). *The Satanic Rituals.* New York: Avon.

LaVey, A. S. (2005 [1969]). *The Satanic Bible.* New York: Avon.

Laycock, J. P. (2020). *Speak of the Devil: How the Satanic Temple Is Changing the Way We Talk About Religion.* Oxford: Oxford University Press.

Laycock, J. P. (2023). *Satanism.* Cambridge: Cambridge University Press.

Leland, C. G. (1899). *Aradia or the Gospel of the Witches.* London: David Nutt.

Lethbridge, T. C. (1962). *Witches: Investigating an Ancient Religion.* London: Routledge and Kegan Paul.

Levack, B. P. (2016). *The Witch-Hunt in Early Modern Europe.* 4th ed. London: Routledge.

Lewis, J. R. (2003). *Legitimating New Religions.* New Brunswick, NJ: Rutgers University Press.

Lincoln, B. (2006). *Holy Terrors: Thinking About Religion after September 11.* 2nd ed. Chicago, IL: University of Chicago Press.

Lipscomb, S. (2021). Why Are Women Becoming Witches? *UnHerd*, 22 May. https://unherd.com/2021/05/why-are-women-becoming-witches/ (accessed 26 June 2023).

Lloyd, M. G. (2012). *Bull of Heaven: The Mythic Life of Eddie Buczynski and the Rise of the New York Pagan.* Hubbardston, MA: Asphodel Press.

Luhrmann, T. M. (1989). *Persuasions of the Witch's Craft: Ritual Magic in Contemporary England.* Cambridge, MA: Harvard University Press.

Machielsen, J. (2021). *The War on Witchcraft: Andrew Dickson White, George Lincoln Burr, and the Origins of Witchcraft Historiography.* Cambridge: Cambridge University Press.

Magliocco, S. (2004). *Witching Culture: Folklore and Neo-Paganism in America.* Philadelphia, PN: University of Pennsylvania Press.

Magliocco, S. (2020). Witchcraft as Political Resistance: Magical Responses to the 2016 Presidential Election in the United States. *Nova Religio: The Journal of Alternative and Emergent Religions*, 23(4), 43–68.

McCormack, C. (2015). Review: MX JUSTIN VIVIAN BOND . . . And Things of THAT Nature! *Broadway World*, 16 September. https://bit.ly/3RlK1NF (accessed 26 June 2023).

Mencej, M. (2017). *Styrian Witches in European Perspective: Ethnographic Fieldwork*. London: Palgrave Macmillan.

Michelet, J. (1992 [1939]). *Satanism and Witchcraft: The Classic Study of Medieval Superstition*. Translated by A. R. Allinson. New York: Carol Publishing.

Miller, C. (2022). How Modern Witches Enchant TikTok: Intersections of Digital, Consumer, and Material Culture(s) on #WitchTok. *Religions*, *13*(2), 1–22.

Monter, E. W. (1972). The Historiography of European Witchcraft: Progress and Prospects. *Journal of Interdisciplinary History*, *2*(4), 435–51.

Morgan, L. (2013). *A Deed Without a Name: Unearthing the Legacy of Traditional Witchcraft*. Winchester: Moon Books.

Mueller, M. (2017). The Chalice and the Rainbow: Conflicts between Women's Spirituality and Transgender Rights in US Wicca in the 2010s. In I. Bårdsen Tøllefsen & C. Giudice, eds., *Female Leaders in New Religious Movements*. Cham: Palgrave Macmillan, 249–78.

Murray, M. (1921). *The Witch-Cult in Western Europe: A Study in Anthropology*. Oxford: Clarendon Press.

Murray, M. (1952). *The God of the Witches*. 2nd ed. London: Faber and Faber.

Oates, S. (2016). *The Star Crossed Serpent III: The Taper That Lights the Way*. Oxford: Mandrake of Oxford.

Ochoa, T. R. (2010). *Society of the Dead: Quita Manaquita and Palo Praise in Cuba*. Berkeley, CA: University of California Press.

O'Doherty, I. (2020). Witch Hunt Against Rowling Shows the Mob Is Never Happy, *Irish Independent*, 11 July. https://bit.ly/3R2ZP6B (accessed 26 June 2023).

O'Neill, B. (2019). The Witch-Hunting of JK Rowling. *Spiked*, 20 December. www.spiked-online.com/2019/12/20/the-witch-hunting-of-jk-rowling/ (accessed 26 June 2023).

Orion, L. (1995). *Never Again the Burning Times: Paganism Revisited*. Long Grove, IL: Waveland Press.

Orrell, E. (2019). 'I Just Like Thinking About the Moon and Lighting Candles': 21st Century Witches on Instagram. *Ethnographic Encounters*, *10*(1), 6–12.

Ortiz Fernández, F. (1906). *Los negros brujos [The Black Witches]*. Madrid: Libreria de Fernando Fé.

Otto, B.-C. (2016). Historicising 'Western Learned Magic': Preliminary Remarks. *Aries: Journal for the Study of Western Esotericism*, *16*(2), 161–240.

Otto, B.-C., & Stausberg, M. (2014 [2013]). General Introduction. In B.-C. Otto & M. Stausberg, eds. *Defining Magic: A Reader*. London: Routledge, 1–13.

Pearson, J. (2002). Witches and Wicca. In J. Pearson, ed. *Belief Beyond Boundaries: Wicca, Celtic Spirituality and the New Age*. Aldershot: Ashgate, 133–72.

Pérez, E. (2021). The Black Atlantic Metaphysics of Azealia Banks: Brujx Womanism at the Kongo Crossroads. *Hypatia: A Journal of Feminist Philosophy, 36*, 519–246.

Powell, T. (2017). *The Witches Ways in the Welsh Borders: Ethnography of Contemporary and Historical Customs of Cunning Folk Magic*. Forest of Dean: Airheart Publishing.

Purkiss, D. (1996). *The Witch in History: Early Modern and Twentieth-Century Representations*. London: Routledge.

Quaglia, S. (2019). Women Are Invoking the Witch to Find Their Power in a Patriarchal Society. *Quartz*, 31 October. https://bit.ly/3GjBYe2 (accessed 26 June 2023).

Quinn, D. (2016). Azealia Banks Cleans Blood-Stained Room She's Used to Practice Witchcraft for 3 Years: 'Real Witches Do Real Things'. *People*, 30 December. https://bit.ly/3uE1fgk (accessed 26 June 2023).

Ramgopal, L. (2016). 'Go and Reclaim Your Tools': Meet the Woman Behind Black Witch University. *Vice*, 4 October. https://bit.ly/3R1Vocb (accessed 26 June 2023).

Rasbold, K. (2020). *The Sacred Art of Brujería: A Path of Healing and Magic*. Woodbury, MN: Llewellyn.

Reilly, P. J. (2018). Lesbians Want a Church of Their Own and IRS Approves. *Forbes*, 3 August. https://bit.ly/47Qt6YW (accessed 26 June 2023).

Robbins, R. H. (1959). *The Encyclopedia of Witchcraft and Demonology*. New York: Crown.

Romberg, R. (2003). *Witchcraft and Welfare: Spiritual Capital and the Business of Magic in Modern Puerto Rico*. Austin, TX: University of Texas Press.

Rose, E. (1962). *A Razor for a Goat: Problems in the History of Witchcraft and Diabolism*. Toronto: University of Toronto Press.

Rountree, K. (2004). *Embracing the Witch and the Goddess: Feminist Ritual-Makers in New Zealand*. London: Routledge.

Rowling, J. K. (2020). [Twitter] 22 September. https://bit.ly/46KQFBK (accessed 26 June 2023).

Ruelas, V. (2022). *The Mexican Witch Lifestyle: Brujeria Spells, Tarot, and Crystal Magic*. New York: Simon Element.

Salomonsen, J. (2002). *Enchanted Feminism: The Reclaiming Witches of San Francisco*. London: Routledge.

Samuel, S. (2018). The Witches of Baltimore. *The Atlantic*, 5 November. https://bit.ly/47XkpvU (accessed 26 June 2023).

Scarre, G., & Callow, J. (2001). *Witchcraft and Magic in Sixteenth- and Seventeenth-Century Europe.* 2nd ed. Basingstoke: Palgrave.

Semmens, J. (2010). Bucca Redivivus: History, Folklore and the Construction of Ethnic Identity Within Modern Pagan Witchcraft in Cornwall. *Cornish Studies, 18*, 141–61.

Sessums, K. (2019). The Chat: Justin Vivian Bond and James Cameron Mitchell. *Sessums Magazine*, 26 June. https://bit.ly/3uAUThH (accessed 26 June 2023).

Sheppard, K. L. (2013). *The Life of Margaret Alice Murray: A Woman's Work in Archaeology.* Lanham, MD: Lexington.

Smith, J. Z. (2004). *Relating Religion: Essays in the Study of Religion.* Chicago, IL: University of Chicago Press.

Sollée, K. J. (2017). *Witches, Sluts, Feminists: Conjuring the Sex Positive.* Berkeley, CA: ThreeL Media.

Starhawk (1979). *The Spiral Dance: A Rebirth of the Ancient Religion of the Great Goddess.* San Francisco, CA: Harper and Row.

Starhawk (1987). *Truth or Dare: Encounters with Power, Authority, and Mystery.* New York: HarperCollins.

Steele, T. (2001). *The Rites and Rituals of Traditional Witchcraft.* Milverton: Capall Bann.

Styers, R. (2004). *Making Magic: Religion, Magic, and Science in the Modern World.* Oxford: Oxford University Press.

Summers, M. (1926). *The History of Witchcraft and Demonology.* New York: Alfred A. Knopf.

Sutin, L. (2000). *Do What Thou Wilt: A Life of Aleister Crowley.* New York: St Martin's Press.

Taliesin (1965a). 'Ancients' and 'Moderns'. *Pentagram, 3*, 9.

Taliesin (1965b). Response to 'Taliesin Attacked … Gardner Defended'. *Pentagram, 5*, 18–9.

Thomas, A. (2022). Free Zone Scientology: An Interview with Dr Aled Thomas. *World Religions and Spirituality Project.* https://bit.ly/3sY1KkW (accessed 26 June 2023).

Tosenberger, C. (in press). The Devil You Know: Reclaiming the Ambivalent Witch in Modern Traditional Witchcraft. In M. D. Foster & J. A. Tolbert, eds., *Möbius Media: Popular Culture, Folklore, and the Folkloresque.* Logan, UT: Utah State University Press.

Townsend Warner, S. (1926). *Lolly Willowes.* London: Chatto & Windus.

Tully, C. (2017). The Artifice of Daidalos: Modern Minoica as Religious Focus in Contemporary Paganism. *International Journal for the Study of New Religions*, *8*(2), 183–212.

Tylor, E. B. (1903). *Primitive Culture – Volume I*. 4th ed. London: John Murray.

Urban, H. B. (2005). *Magia Sexualis: Sex, Magic and Liberation in Modern Western Esotericism*. Berkeley, CA: University of California Press.

Valiente, D. (1989). *The Rebirth of Witchcraft*. London: Robert Hale.

Van Luijk, R. (2016). *Children of Lucifer: The Origins of Modern Religious Satanism*. Oxford: Oxford University Press.

VICE Life (2021). Why Some Black Women Are Turning to Witchcraft. *YouTube*, 18 May. www.youtube.com/watch?v=5qospq0cTw0 (accessed 26 June 2023).

Victor, J. S. (1993). *Satanic Panic: The Creation of a Contemporary Legend*. Chicago, IL: Open Court.

Wallace, D. (2012). Restricted Access: Healers, Heretics and Witches: African Diviners and Pagan Witches Contest the Boundaries of Religion and Magic in Africa. In A. Cheira, ed., *RePresenting Magic, UnDoing Evil: Of Human Inner Light and Darkness*. Leiden: Brill, 39–48.

Wallace, D. (2017). Pagan Identity Politics, Witchcraft, and the Law: Encounters with Postcolonial Nationalism in Democratic South Africa. In K. Rountree, ed., *Cosmopolitanism, Nationalism, and Modern Paganism*. New York: Palgrave Macmillan, 179–99.

Wallace, L. (2017). Trans and Intersex Witches Are Casting Out the Gender Binary. *Them*, 30 October. www.them.us/story/trans-and-intersex-witches (accessed 26 June 2023).

Ward, T. P. (2018). For Members of the Pussy Church of Witchcraft, 'Our Bodies Are the Church'. *The Wild Hunt*, 22 August. Archived at https://bit.ly/3R4UXhv (accessed 26 June 2023).

Waters, T. (2019). *Cursed Britain: A History of Witchcraft and Black Magic in Modern Times*. New Haven, CT: Yale University Press.

Wheatley, D. (1970 [1934]). *The Devil Rides Out*. London: Arrow.

Wheeler, G. J. (2018). An Esbat Among the Quads: An Episode of Witchcraft at Oxford University in the 1920s. *The Pomegranate: The International Journal of Pagan Studies*, *20*(2), 157–78.

Whitmore, B. (2010). *Trials of the Moon: Reopening the Case for Historical Witchcraft*. Auckland: Briar Books.

Whitney, E. (1995). The Witch 'She'/The Historian 'He': Gender and the Historiography of the European Witch-Hunts. *Journal of Women's History*, *7*(3), 77–101.

Ziegler, R. (2012). *Satanism, Magic and Mysticism in Fin-de-siècle France.* Basingstoke: Palgrave Macmillan.

Films, Television, and Podcasts

American Horror Story: Coven. 2013–2014. [Television]. USA: FX.

Buffy the Vampire Slayer. 1997–2003. [Television]. USA: The WB and UPN.

Charmed. 1998–2006. [Television]. USA: The WB.

Charmed. 2018–2020. [Television]. USA: The CW.

Chilling Adventures of Sabrina. 2018–2020. [Television]. USA: Netflix.

Juju: The Web Series. 2019. [Web Television]. USA.

Sabrina the Teenage Witch. 1996–2003. [Television]. USA: ABC and the WB.

Suspiria. 1977. [Film]. Dario Argento. Dir. Italy: Seda Spettacoli.

The Blair Witch Project. 1999. [Film]. Daniel Myrick and Eduardo Sánchez. Dir. USA: Haxan Films.

The Craft. 1996. [Film]. Andrew Fleming. Dir. USA: Columbia Pictures.

The Craft: Legacy. 2020. [Film]. Zoe Lister-Jones. Dir. USA: Columbia Pictures, Blumhouse Productions, and Red Wagon Entertainment.

The Love Witch. 2016. [Film]. Anna Biller. Dir. USA: Anna Biller Productions.

The Witch. 2015. [Film]. Robert Eggers. Dir. USA and Canada: Parts and Labor, RT Features, Rooks Nest Entertainment, Maiden Voyage Pictures, Mott Street Pictures, Code Red Productions, Scythia Films, Pulse Films, and Special Projects.

The Witch Trials of J. K. Rowling. 2023. [Podcast]. USA: The Free Press.

Songs

Anohni (2012). Future Feminism. Antony and the Johnsons. *Cut the World.* [CD]. Rough Trade Records.

Bond, J. V. (2011a). Crowley à la Lee. Justin Vivian Bond. *Dendrophile.* [CD]. Weatherbox.

Bond, J. V. (2011b). The New Economy. Justin Vivian Bond. *Dendrophile.* [CD]. Weatherbox.

Princess Nokia (2017). Brujas. Princess Nokia. *1992 Deluxe.* [CD]. Rough Trade Records.

Zebra Katz (2013). BLK WICCAN. Zebra Katz. DRKLNG. [Download]. ZFK Records.

Acknowledgements

Of course, there are tens if not hundreds of people to whom I am grateful for discussing issues of witchcraft, esotericism, and new religions over the years, so my thanks go out to them all, whatever they may think of my published research. When it comes to *The New Witches of the West* specifically, special thanks must go to Rebecca Moore for inviting me to contribute to this Element series and then for offering her thoughts on the completed manuscript. She has always been wonderful to work with. Thanks also to Christopher Josiffe for offering confirmation on certain points regarding the fascinating Rollo Ahmed, and to Paul Cowdell for introducing me to *The Secret of High Eldersham*. My appreciation must also go to the two anonymous peer reviewers for both their time and their very kind comments, as well as to all those involved in the copy-editing and publishing process. Finally, thanks to my nearest and dearest, for putting up with my work on this project and the attendant piles of books that I have inevitably left everywhere.

Cambridge Elements ⁼

New Religious Movements

Founding Editor

†James R. Lewis
Wuhan University

The late James R. Lewis was Professor of Philosophy at Wuhan University, China. He served as the editor or co-editor for four book series, was the general editor for the *Alternative Spirituality and Religion Review,* and the associate editor for the *Journal of Religion and Violence.* His publications include *The Cambridge Companion to Religion and Terrorism* (Cambridge University Press 2017) and *Falun Gong: Spiritual Warfare and Martyrdom* (Cambridge University Press 2018).

Series Editor

Rebecca Moore
San Diego State University

Rebecca Moore is Emerita Professor of Religious Studies at San Diego State University. She has written and edited numerous books and articles on Peoples Temple and the Jonestown tragedy. She has served as co-general editor or reviews editor of *Nova Religio* since 2000. Publications include *Beyond Brainwashing: Perspectives on Cult Violence* (Cambridge University Press 2018) and *Peoples Temple and Jonestown in the Twenty-First Century* (Cambridge University Press 2022).

About the Series

Elements in New Religious Movements go beyond cult stereotypes and popular prejudices to present new religions and their adherents in a scholarly and engaging manner. Case studies of individual groups, such as Transcendental Meditation and Scientology, provide in-depth consideration of some of the most well known, and controversial, groups. Thematic examinations of women, children, science, technology, and other topics focus on specific issues unique to these groups. Historical analyses locate new religions in specific religious, social, political, and cultural contexts. These examinations demonstrate why some groups exist in tension with the wider society and why others live peaceably in the mainstream. The series highlights the differences, as well as the similarities, within this great variety of religious expressions. To discuss contributing to this series please contact Professor Moore, remoore@sdsu.edu.

Cambridge Elements ≡

New Religious Movements